Tackling
Addiction

of related interest

Substance Misuse
The Implications of Research, Policy and Practice
Edited by Joy Barlow
ISBN 978 1 84310 696 8
Research Highlights in Social Work Series

Trauma, Drug Misuse and Transforming Identities
A Life Story Approach
Kim Etherington
Foreword by Monty Don
ISBN 978 1 84310 493 3

Drug Addiction and Families
Marina Barnard
Foreword by Fergal Keane
ISBN 978 1 84310 403 2

Therapeutic Communities for the Treatment of Drug Users
Edited by Barbara Rawlings and Rowdy Yates
ISBN 978 1 85302 817 5
Community, Culture and Changes Series

Recovery from Depression Using the Narrative Approach
A Guide for Doctors, Complementary Therapists and Mental Health Professionals
Damien Ridge
ISBN 978 1 84310 575 6

Understanding Street Drugs
A Handbook of Substance Misuse for Parents, Teachers and Other Professionals
2nd Edition
David Emmet and Graeme Nice
ISBN 978 1 84310 351 6

Getting Wise to Drugs
A Resource for Teaching Children about Drugs, Dangerous Substances and Other Risky Situations
David Emmet and Graeme Nice
ISBN 978 1 84310 507 7

Tackling Addiction

Pathways to Recovery

Edited by Rowdy Yates and Margaret S. Malloch

Jessica Kingsley Publishers
London and Philadelphia

First published in 2010
by Jessica Kingsley Publishers
116 Pentonville Road
London N1 9JB, UK
and
400 Market Street, Suite 400
Philadelphia, PA 19106, USA

www.jkp.com

Copyright © Jessica Kingsley Publishers 2010

Crown copyright material is reproduced with the permission of
the Controller of HMSO and the Queen's Printer for Scotland.

Library of Congress Cataloging in Publication Data
Tackling addiction : pathways to recovery / edited by Rowdy Yates and Margaret S. Malloch.
p. cm.
ISBN 978-1-84905-017-3 (alk. paper)
1. Drug addiction--Treatment--Great Britain. 2. Therapeutic communities--Great Britain.
I. Yates, Rowdy, 1950- II. Malloch, Margaret S.
HV5801.T24 2010
616.86'06--dc22
2009038484

British Library Cataloguing in Publication Data
A CIP catalogue record for this book is available from the British Library

ISBN 978 1 84905 017 3

Printed and bound in Great Britain by
MPG Books Ltd, Cornwall

Contents

Figures and Tables

Acknowledgements

We would like to thank all our contributors to both this book and to the Pathways to Recovery seminar series. Particular thanks go to the Foundation for the Sociology for Health and Illness for funding the seminar series. This was a journey for us too and one in which we found ourselves often humbled by the courage and perseverance of those recovered and recovering individuals in whose footsteps we followed.

Introduction

Margaret S. Malloch and Rowdy Yates

This book arose from our interest, both academic and personal, in the increasing attention given to 'recovery' as a way forward for drug policy in Scotland and beyond. While it would be fair to say that recovery has always been implicated, either centrally or on the periphery, of interventions in the drug and alcohol field, it has only recently been embraced by government as a key policy focus and placed at the forefront of policy documents. Our own work in this field, and that of our contributors, evidenced that 'recovery' was being increasingly discussed in areas where it had previously been ignored or overlooked. But this emphasis on recovery did not always seem tangible; it was difficult to grasp what people who were talking about recovery actually meant by the term and the translation of this concept into practice seemed even more elusive. While some commentators welcomed the potential for a new paradigm in drug and alcohol services, others saw the attention placed on 'recovery' to be a cynical exercise in moralizing and, potentially, a cost-cutting exercise. At the same time, it was evident that people who were 'in recovery' or who described themselves in this way were less ambiguous about what it meant for them and how it shaped their lives. Our attempt to capture the shifting sands of this agenda led to the Pathways to Recovery seminar series from which this book emerged. We hope that by bringing together the thoughts and views of academics, practitioners and people in recovery, we will add something to the ongoing debate.

This book is very relevant at this time in Scotland, as well as nationally and internationally. The Scottish Government has identified 'recovery' as a key element of the new Drugs Strategy and this concept has formed a key element of both the Scottish Advisory Committee on

Drug Misuse (SACDM)'s *Essential Care* report (2008) and the Scottish Government's own strategy document: *Road to Recovery* (2008). We are aware that developments in Scotland are being observed with interest by practitioners and policy makers in other countries.

Context

While the UK Government's ten-year Drugs Strategy, *Drugs: Protecting Families and Communities* (HM Government 2008) has continued to prioritize crime reduction and community safety, the United Kingdom Drug Policy Commission (UKDPC 2008) emphasized the importance of 'recovery', which it set out to mean: 'voluntary sustained control over substance use which maximises health and wellbeing and participation in the rights, roles and responsibilities of society' (p.6).

In the US, recovery is emphasized in both policy objectives and outcome measures (Laudet 2007, 2008) although the meaning of recovery has remained somewhat ambiguous. To try to clarify this, the Betty Ford Institute convened a Consensus Panel with the aim of providing an 'initial' definition of recovery (Betty Ford Institute Consensus Panel 2007). The panel noted that 'recovery from substance dependence is a voluntarily maintained lifestyle characterized by sobriety, personal health and citizenship' (p.221). While acknowledged as a starting point in defining recovery, even this broad definition has raised a number of concerns (Arndt and Taylor 2007).

Recovery has taken a central role in the latest Scottish Drug Strategy (Scottish Government 2008) tellingly entitled *The Road to Recovery: A New Approach to Tackling Scotland's Drug Problem*. Here, recovery is defined as 'a process through which an individual is enabled to move on from their problem drug use towards a drug-free life and become an active and contributing member of society' (p.vi). The SACDM has also published a report 'on the approach required to maximise opportunity for recovery from problem substance use in Scotland' (SACDM 2008, p.1).

The ongoing debates that have taken place in Scotland and elsewhere around the meaning of recovery and how it should be obtained and/ or sustained stem from a lack of clarity not only around recovery, but also around the meanings of addiction and dependence. This has been further confused by the long-standing polarization of maintenance or substitute prescribing (sometimes referred to as supported recovery) and abstinence, which has been a spectre in drug treatment debates since the 1980s and indeed, earlier. The work of William White has been important in highlighting and informing current debate in this area (White 1990, 2000, 2007).

While it has been widely accepted that recovery is an individual process where the person in recovery is able to define what recovery and what 'living well' means to them – that is, a perception rather than a model – there are clearly implications in pursuing recovery as a policy objective. For example, what constitutes 'success'? What is the difference between 'sustained' and 'treated' recovery? How is recovery actually understood? What resources (social, political and economic) are needed to support and maintain recovery? (For example, see Cloud and Granfield 2008.)

While the available evidence is limited, Arndt and Taylor (2007) have highlighted the lack of understanding of the term 'recovery' in the eyes of the majority of the general public (62% of survey respondents believed that someone in recovery 'is trying to stop using alcohol or illicit drugs' (p.275)). While the study they refer to was conducted in the US, there is no reason to think that the concept of recovery is any more clearly understood in the United Kingdom by the general public or indeed policy makers. Nevertheless, the Scottish Drugs Strategy aims to 'set out a new vision where all our drug treatment and rehabilitation services are based on the principle of recovery' (Scottish Government 2008, p.iv).

Background

In October 2007 we received funding from the Foundation for the Sociology of Health and Illness to host a seminar series at the University of Stirling aimed at bringing practitioners, academics and researchers together from health, addiction and criminal justice professions to examine how drug cessation was defined and measured and what significance analyses of 'recovery' could offer to an understanding of individual, institutional and structural concepts of health and well-being.

The proposal was initiated in response to our recognition that increasing levels of 'drug-related crime' had led to innovative interdisciplinary attempts to develop services and interventions aimed at encouraging and enabling individuals to reduce or end their use of drugs. Workers from health, addiction and criminal justice services now work together to provide interventions aimed to reduce drug-related offending behaviour. However, we recognized that this emphasis on 'fast-track' treatment through the criminal justice system, with an emphasis on 'coerced treatment', failed to take account of 'recovery' as a long-term and ongoing process. Indeed, as more people accessed treatment through the criminal justice system, it seemed that the option for abstinence-based provision was curtailed (McIvor *et al.* 2006), while innovative projects located within criminal justice often struggled to maintain 'recovery' as an outcome in the face of pressure to measure success through rates of reconviction and reduced offending (Loucks *et al.* 2006).

The seminar series aimed to consider concerns that the increasing dominance of substitute prescribing in the treatment arena obscured the possibilities offered by other approaches, with the notion of 'drug-free recovery' disappearing from the treatment agenda. The seminars provided an opportunity to bring together major figures in treatment and research to present their views and evidence. Each seminar addressed a specific approach to recovery and considered the relationship of these approaches to the broader policy context.

It became clear that this debate was characterized by differences in opinion, variations in ideological and philosophical position and that too often the voices of people in recovery were overlooked. Many of the individuals who describe themselves as 'in recovery' have found support through mutual aid societies and have often gone on to work with others to 'give something back' as well as to bolster their own recovery. Their experiences present a powerful challenge to some of the assumptions which underpin time-limited interventions and pessimistic diagnoses of addiction. We provide examples of individual 'voices of recovery', where emphasis is placed on the importance of an holistic approach to the individual and understanding recovery as a process of change which affects the physical, emotional, mental and spiritual realms of life. In many ways this presents a real challenge to the operation of traditional and/or statutory services. Some of the individuals who share their experiences here have gone on to work in the field of addiction while others have not. Those who have often present an ongoing challenge to the more traditional service provisions and have used the benefits of their own experiences to support others in their recovery. These voices are set out in interview format to remain true to the contributors.

The chapters raise a number of issues: reflections on what recovery means and examining the role of recovery groups and communities (Yates and Malloch in Chapter 1, Best in Chapter 2, and Gilman and Yates in Chapter 6); changing practice and supporting recovery within projects

(Kuladharini in Chapter 3); the challenge of obtaining funds and support for projects which do not come under the rubric of 'professional' services (Bryce and Edwards in Chapter 8). Recovery in therapeutic communities is examined (De Leon in Chapter 5) and its application in practice is considered by drawing on the Ley Community experience (Dawson and Zandvoort in Chapter 7). We consider the importance of diversity (Thom in Chapter 4), replicated in the experiences of our respondents in Chapter 8. The implications for clinical practice are outlined (Kidd in Chapter 9), what we are to make of the political context within which these debates are played out (Stevens in Chapter 10) and what this offers to our understanding of 'coerced' treatment (McSweeney in Chapter 11). We bring together some of the key themes and potential ways forward in our concluding chapter (Chapter 12).

The Pathways to Recovery seminar series helped engage practitioners, academics and policy makers around this issue, as well as informing individuals with a tangential interest in the area of addiction and recovery. We hope this book will make a significant further contribution to the theoretical, practical and policy analysis centring on discussions of current developments in addiction policy and practice. It is particularly relevant given the topicality of the subject and the range of experts who have contributed chapters. Specifically, it is unique in bringing together contributions from professionals working in the field; academics and researchers; and individuals who define themselves as being 'in recovery'. It is our intention that it will inform ongoing discussion and debate about the way forward for policy and practice in this area.

References

Arndt, S. and Taylor, P. (2007) 'Commentary on "Defining and measuring 'recovery'".' *Journal of Substance Abuse Treatment 33*, 275–276.

Betty Ford Institute Consensus Panel (2007) 'What is recovery? A working definition from the Betty Ford Institute.' *Journal of Substance Abuse Treatment 33*, 221–228.

Cloud, W. and Granfield, R. (2008) 'Conceptualizing recovery capital: Expansion of a theoretical construct.' *Substance Use and Misuse 43*, 1971–1986.

HM Government (2008) *Drugs: Protecting Families and Communities. Action Plan 2008–11*. London: Home Office.

Laudet, A. (2007) 'What does recovery mean to you: Lessons from the recovery experience for research and practice.' *Journal of Substance Abuse Treatment 33*, 243–256.

Laudet, A. (2008) 'The road to recovery: Where are we going and how do we get there? Empirically driven conclusions and future directions for service development and research.' *Substance Use and Misuse 43*, 2001–2020.

Loucks, N., Malloch, M., McIvor, G. and Gelsthorpe, L. (2006) *Evaluation of the 218 Centre*. Edinburgh: Scottish Executive.

McIvor, G., Barnsdale, L., Eley, S., Malloch, M., Yates, R. and Brown, A. (2006) *The Operation and Effectiveness of Glasgow and Fife Drug Court Pilots.* Edinburgh: Scottish Executive.

Scottish Advisory Committee on Drug Misuse (SACDM) (2008) *Essential Care: A Report on the Approach Required to Maximise Opportunity for Recovery from Problem Substance Use in Scotland.* Edinburgh: SACDM.

Scottish Government (2008) *The Road to Recovery: A New Approach to Tackling Scotland's Drug Problem.* Edinburgh: Scottish Government.

United Kingdom Drug Policy Commission (UKDPC) (2008) *A Vision of Recovery.* London: UKDPC.

White, W. (1990) *Pathways from the Culture of Addiction to the Culture of Recovery,* 2nd edn. Center City, MN: Hazelden Publishing.

White, W. (2000) 'Toward a new recovery movement: Historical reflections on recovery, treatment and advocacy.' Recovery Community Support Program Conference, *Working Together for Recovery,* 3–5 April 2000, Arlington, VA.

White, W. (2007) 'Addiction recovery: Its definition and conceptual boundaries.' *Journal of Substance Abuse Treatment 33,* 229–241.

CHAPTER 1

The Road Less Travelled? A Short History of Addiction Recovery

Rowdy Yates and Margaret S. Malloch

Introduction

Some 40 years ago, Chuck Dederich, founder-director of Synanon, the first addiction therapeutic community, famously remarked to a new resident, 'Today is the first day of the rest of your life'. The remark went on to be one of the more memorable 'concepts' of the early therapeutic community movement. Dederich would have had no way of knowing that this remark would also become a 'kiss-me-quick' slogan found alongside a range of trite sayings and homilies on sale in thousands of tourist sales outlets and airport novelty shops, with no understanding of the serious issues referred to in the original. For that at least, we feel, he can be forgiven (Rawlings and Yates 2001).

Dederich's meaning was clear. Take stock. Go back, find out what went wrong and fix it. Stop. Rewind. Replay. The notion of calling a halt to a pattern of futile and self-destructive behaviour, of coming to an understanding of what drives that behaviour and changing it, overcoming it, is hundreds of years old. Traditionally, we have called it 'recovery' although, for many, the term 'discovery' may be more apposite.

It seems strange then, that 'recovery' remains, for many, a controversial area of addiction treatment, with many involved in mainstream specialist treatment expressing doubts as to both its efficacy and even advisability (Day *et al.* 2005). In large part, this dubiety reflects our cultural and historical understanding of addiction and its consistent medicalization over two centuries. Peele (1995) has noted that the vigorous promotion of alcoholism as a chronic, relapsing disease by the scientific medical community in the 1950s and 1960s (Glatt 1952; Jellinek 1952, 1960; Keller 1962) has effectively embedded the notion of addiction, in both the public consciousness and (to a lesser, though significant extent) within academic discourse, as an incurable condition which can, at best, be managed and contained. Room (1983) has charted the opposition to this position by sociological researchers and proponents of the behaviourist schools but, although these arguments gained significant ground during the 1970s and early 1980s, the increasing focus, during the past two decades, upon infection control and crime reduction has resulted in a general return to a medical model of addiction treatment predicated upon the management of the problem and containment of its physiological and societal symptoms (Ashton 2008; Yates 1999b, 2002).

However, in more recent years, there appears to have been a growing interest both in a wider view of addiction and its treatment in general and of the issue of recovery in particular (Betty Ford Institute Consensus Panel 2007; HM Government 2008; Scottish Government 2008). In part, this rebirth of interest in recovery appears to have been driven by a media-led dissatisfaction with the perceived failures of the substitute prescribing policy of the previous two decades (Ashton 2008). In part also, though, it appears to owe much to a largely grassroots-led movement to redefine the nature and direction of the treatment process (Bamber and Best 2009). This chapter briefly charts the historical trajectory of addiction, addiction treatment and recovery and considers the antecedents of this 'new recovery movement'.

The discovery of addiction

McCormick (1969), Levine (1978, 1984), Room (2003) and others have all remarked upon the dearth of references to 'alcoholism' or 'addiction' prior to the birth of the industrial revolution, both in Europe and America. Room and Levine, in particular, have speculated on the cultural specificity of the 'addiction' concept. Levine, using a similar analytical approach to Foucault's examination of mental disorder, argues that the industrialization of America at the beginning of the nineteenth century established a cultural context within which it was possible, even necessary, to define certain types of drinking behaviour – which had previously been seen in terms of personal preference and excited little comment – as an affliction of the will.

McCormick, discussing representations of drinking in the novels of Smollett, Fielding, Dickens and Gaskell, notes, 'When we look at fiction about 1830, when the industrial revolution was in full swing, we find that the same drinking may be described as existed 80 years before but that a new and more desperate kind of solitary, tragic and inexplicable drinking has come into existence beside it' (1969, p.959).

The notion of a disease, which robs those afflicted with it of their individual will, is embedded in a cultural context where individuality and liberty is a paramount aspiration and where appropriate behaviour is an individual personal responsibility. This, of course, is precisely the cultural matrix which developed with the industrialization of previously rural communities, where controls had tended to be vested more explicitly within the family or 'tribe' than with the individual.

These concepts have proved to be of an enduring nature. The current definition of addiction or dependence, as set out in the *International Classification of Diseases* (ICD-10) (World Health Organization 1992), neatly sets out this diagnostic requirement as, 'Impaired capacity to control substance-taking behaviour in terms of onset, termination or level of use'. ICD-10 lists a number of other manifestations of addiction,[1] including a preoccupation with the substance of choice, which disregards other important concerns or alternatives. Room argues that this definition again, is culturally specific, relating to a social structure in which time has become a commodity in itself, 'a cultural frame in which time is… used or spent rather than simply experienced' (2003, p.226).

Thus, the discovery of addiction (and, consequently, of 'recovery') came during a period of extraordinary social upheaval and change. In America, in particular, the period was also associated with additional changes in established communities as existing residents moved out to explore and settle new territories and were replaced by significant numbers of immigrants from mainland Europe and Ireland. In the period between 1785 and 1835 the population of the US almost doubled (Peele 1995). In the newly settled territories drinking houses were largely rudimentary, frequented by prostitutes and gamblers, and generally structured to encourage drunkenness and heavy drink-related spending; a far cry from the community-oriented taverns in the close-knit communities most

---

1   The World Health Organization uses the term 'dependence' – currently the preferred terminology.

settlers had left behind. In the cities and established communities the new immigrants brought with them European drinking practices, which were often frowned upon and largely misunderstood.

If the birth of the emergent temperance and recovery movements were set against both changes in drinking patterns and significant, corresponding changes in social structure and demographics, it is perhaps not surprising that these movements were almost always white, Protestant, anti-Catholic and, often, anti-immigrant. The Reverend Burchard's denunciation of the Democrats as, 'the party of rum, Romanism, and rebellion!' was echoed by much of the temperance writing of that time (Gusfield 1963). In the UK, too, there was an air of intolerance within the temperance movement, which went well beyond its abhorrence of drink and drunkenness. In the late nineteenth century many Scottish temperance organizations added ice cream to their list of items to be castigated, presumably both because it was made by Catholic Italian immigrants and because it afforded more pleasure than a Scottish Calvinist was prepared to contemplate (King 1979; Yates and McIvor 2003). Early in the twentieth century some UK temperance movements similarly turned their ire on the new fashion for moving-picture houses (Longmate 1968).

This religious intolerance within the emergent temperance and recovery movements is understandable. The loss of control, identified by these movements as a classic characteristic of addiction, can be seen as a secularized continuation of an affliction long identified by established religion as the primary threat to spiritual awakening. Inglis (1975) and others (Room 2001, 2003; Yates 1999b) have noted that the popular conception of addiction as an external force which exerts its will over the individual against his or her will is redolent of an earlier belief in possession by devils. Little wonder then that the early writing of the temperance and recovery movements cited the 'devil in the bottle' and the 'demon drink' as the central object of their loathing and fear.

The early temperance and recovery movements

The temperance and recovery movements which emerged (both in the US and the UK) in the first half of the nineteenth century tended to be an amorphous mix of recovery community and anti-alcohol campaigning body. It is difficult to separate the two movements and often the membership of a particular organization was an eclectic mixture of the two. The Anti-Saloon League and the American Temperance Society in the US and the Independent Order of Rechabites and the Band of Hope in the UK, for instance, welcomed membership from both prohibitionist campaigners and 'reformed drunkards' (the term 'alcoholic' was largely unused until the beginnings of the twentieth century).

However, this was not always the case. The Washingtonians (more formally entitled the Washington Temperance Society), a recovery movement founded in 1840 by a group of former drinkers, eschewed religious doctrine and allowed only 'reformed drunkards' to speak at their meetings (Maxwell 1950; Peele 1995). The Washingtonian meetings followed a format remarkably similar to that adopted by the Alcoholics Anonymous (AA) fellowship almost a hundred years later. T.S. Arthur (1843), in a temperance tract published some eight years after their formation, paints a vivid picture of his attendance at Washingtonian meetings in Philadelphia and offers a series of somewhat romanticized vignettes of the lives and tribulations of some of its members. Even within this short space of time, the Washingtonians were holding regular meetings in most East Coast cities in America and had already established a number of lodging houses for the respite of their fallen members. On the 110th anniversary of the birth of George Washington, Abraham Lincoln chose the meeting of the Springfield Washingtonians to deliver his memorial address (Basler 1953). At its peak, the Washingtonians numbered between 300,000 and 600,000 (reports vary wildly) and could boast at least 150,000 members in long-term recovery (Maxwell 1950; Peele 1995; White 2001).

Although the organization allowed only those in recovery to speak at their meetings, both membership and attendance were open to all. As a result, membership appears to have been swelled by an influx of temperance campaigners and religious proselytizers. This resulted in a series of damaging, and ultimately fatal, internal schisms with some members insisting that the organization be more active in the prohibition campaign, more meaningfully connected to the established church and even more active in the anti-slavery movement. For some 20 years, the Washingtonians flourished, founding new branches across America, but by the 1860s internal feuds caused the organization to implode. Some of its sober houses continued, often under the management of other temperance organizations; the sober house in Chicago became the Washington Hospital and continued to offer alcohol treatment up until the 1980s. But mostly the organization simply crumbled. Members left to join other related bodies and by the 1930s the dissolution was so complete that the founders of AA claimed never to have heard of it (Peele 1995).

Not all the early American recovery movements were to be found in the white Protestant communities. Indeed some of the earliest 'sober circles' appeared amongst the Native American population (White 2000). Both Kenekuk, the so-called Kickapoo prophet, and Handsome Lake, a Seneca chief,[2] founded popular movements in the early nineteenth century (White 2000), built around the concept of recovery and sobriety but extending across much of the cultural life of their tribe (Herring 1877; Parker 1913; White and Whiters 2005). Both Kenekuk and Handsome Lake were reformed drinkers. Both saw sobriety as a first step in restoring cultural integrity and 'upright living' to a people humiliated and disenfranchised by decades of white aggression and deceit. In this they foreshadowed the central tenets of the Black Power movement – similarly led by a reformed criminal and multi-drug user, Malcolm X – over a hundred years later (White and Whiters 2005).

Handsome Lake did much to restore the broken Iroquois Nation and rebuild the confederation as a respected force in Native American politics. His Gaiwiio (Good Message) runs to many pages and was (and still is) learned by heart by many of his followers (Sturtevant and Trigger 1978). A shortened form of the Gaiwiio continues to be recited at certain Iroquois ceremonies each year (Smith 1985). Part of the Gaiwiio reads:

> Now it comes to his mind that perchance evil has arisen because of strong drink and he resolves to use it nevermore. Now he continually thinks of this every day and every hour. Yea, he continually thinks of this. Then a time comes and he craves drink again for he thinks that he can not recover his strength without it. Now two ways he thinks: what once he did and whether he will ever recover. (Parker 1913, p.22)[3]

Whilst many of the early recovery groups often dissipated their energy in political activity, most notably in campaigning for prohibition, this was not always the case. The respite houses established by the Washingtonians provided a template which many organizations adopted. McLaughlin (1989, 1991) has charted the remarkable rise and fall of the inebriates' reformatory and these reformatories in many ways continued where the Washingtonians left off. In the latter half of the nineteenth century,

---

2 The Seneca people were one of the six tribes which constituted the Iroquois Nation.
3 Translated by William Bluesky, a Seneca Indian and Baptist preacher. The translation was verified by Parker with the Seneca Council.

Jerry and Maria McAuley founded the New York City Rescue Mission (Bonner 1990). Jerry McAuley was a former small-time criminal and drunkard who had converted to Christianity whilst serving a 15-year sentence for robbery in Sing Sing. McAuley married Maria in 1872 and in the same year they opened a mission on Water Street as the 'Helping Hand for Men'.[4] This was the first 'soup kitchen' for the 'homeless and undeserving poor', a model which was widely copied in subsequent years, including the well-known Bowery Mission in which McAuley appears to have been peripherally involved (Offord 1970) and the later work of the Salvation Army in America (White and Whiters 2005).

In Europe in general, and the UK in particular, similar developments were emerging (MacLeod 1967). Reformed drinkers in various temperance movements were particularly active in developing alternatives to drinking; so-called sober living activities. In Scotland numerous tea-rooms were opened under temperance management (Yates and McIvor 2003). In Paisley, a Temperance Tower, containing a camera obscura, a tea-room and concert hall and an art gallery, was erected by public subscription. On the Clyde, where Sunday excursions as a result of the Sabbath licensing restrictions (restrictions which did not apply to sea-going vessels) had become somewhat Bacchanalian,[5] the SS Ivanhoe was launched as the world's first temperance boat (Paterson 1969; Yates and McIvor 2003).

The Good Templars, in particular, held regular lodge meetings for 'reformed drunkards' and these attracted huge attendances. The Good Templar Lodge in Airdrie, Scotland was reputed to be the largest in the world, with a membership of 4198 (King 1979). Elsewhere in Europe similar developments were promoting the concept of recovery. Notable amongst these was the Swiss organization Blue Cross (now the International Federation of the Blue Cross or Fédération Internationale de la Croix-Bleue). Founded in 1877, the Blue Cross was soon established in a number of European countries as a forerunner of AA. Indeed, in some European – and later, African – countries, Blue Cross has continued to rival AA as the predominant mutual-aid society (Blocker, Fahey and Tyrrell 2003).

---

4   The Helping Hand for Men Mission appears to have had a number of names. It was most commonly referred to as the 'McAuley Mission' and that is the name which appears above the door in early photographs. It was later renamed the 'New York City Rescue Mission', the name under which it continues to operate: www.nycrescue.org.

5   The Glaswegian expression 'steaming', as a colloquial term for intoxicated, dates from this period.

At the beginning of the twentieth century the Emmanuel Movement, based in the Emmanuel Baptist Church in Boston, Massachusetts, began to attract significant attention for their blend of spirituality, medicine and a kind of basic psychotherapy. The movement attracted serious criticism from Freud during his brief visit to the United States in 1909. Freud was, perhaps understandably, particularly scathing about the limited medical qualifications of the movement's main protagonists (Dubiel 2004). Despite Freud's scepticism and that of many other medical professionals the movement grew and in 1909 Ernest Jacoby began to organize weekly meetings at Emmanuel Church. More meetings began to be established as Jacoby Clubs ('A Club for Men to Help Themselves by Helping Others') and Jacoby Clubs and their weekly meetings flourished throughout the 1920s and 1930s. In Boston the Jacoby Club provided meeting space for one of the earliest AA groups but the two organizations remained separate and the Jacoby Clubs gradually lost out to their newer, more vigorous fellow traveller (McCarthy 1984). The story of the early days of Alcoholics Anonymous has been told many times (Dubiel 2004) and need hardly be reiterated here. The organization was founded in America in 1934 by two former drinkers and, once established, went on to become one of the most widespread and influential mutual aid movements in the addictions field (White 2001).

Disease and recovery in modern times

For most of the nineteenth century and the early years of the twentieth, the central concern was the use and misuse of alcohol. In the middle half of the century, though, this began to change and other so-called 'illicit' drugs became a major cause of concern. The disease model and the popular image of the 'enslaved dope fiend' became common currency and from the 1950s onwards drug policy and specialist addiction treatment services have been dominated by the disease discourse. The publication of Jellinek's (1952) work on phases of alcoholism, and its subsequent incorporation into World Health Organization guidelines (Room 1983), significantly influenced discussions on the nature of addiction and recovery for most of the 1950s and 1960s. This disease model of addiction was not without its critics. Trice and Wahl (1958) tested Jellinek's hypothesis and concluded, 'if the concept of a disease process in alcoholism is valid, only the earliest or the most advanced stages are reliably indicated' (p.636). Similarly, the presentation of alcoholism as an *irreversible* disease has been subjected to much debate and criticism.

Davies (1962) provided an early challenge to this notion with a paper in the *Quarterly Journal of Studies on Alcohol*, which noted the capacity of many of his patients to return to normal drinking patterns. Commentaries in subsequent issues – on both his findings and his diagnostic methodology – were heated but largely scholarly. Not so the response to the Rand Report, *Alcoholism and Treatment* (Armor, Polich and Stambul 1976). The controversy which surrounded the publication of this report, with its finding that not only was a reversion to controlled drinking possible but that it was the most likely successful outcome, sparked a public argument which refused to die down. Room (1983) has noted that some studies of controlled drinking had their funding withdrawn at this time and that the debate became at times extremely emotive. The authors were accused of providing struggling abstainers with a 'scientific excuse for drinking' (Room 1983) and numerous commentators predicted dire consequences as a result of its publication (Roizen 1987). However, as Roizen points out, subsequent studies (Hingson, Scotch and Goldman 1977) indicated that this apprehension had been misplaced and the publication of the report – and its interpretation in the media – had had little or no impact on drinking behaviour.

The impact of these, largely American, debates upon British drug policy and treatment has been extensively considered (Spear 1994, 2002; Yates 2002). The late 1950s and early 1960s was a time when the UK was reluctantly, and often resentfully, taking its lead from the US in a great many things. World War II had left the UK deeply in debt, economically and politically, to the US. In coming to terms with the dissolution of its empire, it was perhaps not surprising that the UK should implicitly acknowledge America's greater experience in a number of – mainly technological – areas whilst remaining contemptuous of her lack of tradition and frightened of her apparently alien culture.

Although there were a number of agencies – both medical and non-medical – providing services of varying kinds to drug users in the 1960s (Turner 1994; Yates 2002), it is probably fair to say that these were largely independent, isolated interventions and the beginnings of an identifiable British drug treatment network did not truly emerge until after the publication of the Government report, *Drug Addiction: The Second Report of the Interdepartmental Committee* (HM Government 1965). When it did, it almost inevitably reflected popular conceptions about the nature of addiction and concentrated almost exclusively on heroin and cocaine, the 'American disease' (Yates 1999a).

As in the 1920s (Kohn 1992), lurid and wholly inaccurate films, sensationalizing drugs – particularly heroin – had caught the imagination of huge audiences. Most of these films were American-produced; perhaps the best known *The Man with the Golden Arm* starring Frank Sinatra (Shapiro 2005), with its portrayal of addiction as both inevitable and irreversible. Around this time also, an agreement between the UK Musicians' Union and its US counterpart opened the door to exchanges of musicians; particularly jazz musicians, many of whom were notorious for their drug consumption. In a well-publicized raid in the mid-1950s London police arrested Ronnie Scott (for possession of cocaine) and a number of other musicians at his jazz club (Clayson 1995; Shapiro 1988).

Drugs were rapidly becoming associated with America (and with jazz). And drugs meant heroin and cocaine. Thus when the Second Brain Report[6] concentrated exclusively upon these two drugs and ignored the burgeoning use of amphetamine-type drugs and cannabis, there were few, if any, dissenting voices (Spear 2002).

In the long term, though, this decision was to have a stultifying effect upon the development of the drugs treatment network in the UK. Inevitably, the remit of the 'drug dependency units' (DDUs) recommended by Brain was limited to heroin and cocaine and the early decision, taken jointly by London DDU consultants, not to prescribe cocaine further limited the remit (Mitcheson 1994). Perhaps more surprisingly the emerging voluntary sector too became almost entirely focused upon injectable opiates.

Even outside London (and it should be remembered that treatment service, like policy, was largely London-oriented) the small number of voluntary sector agencies dealing with drug users were, by the mid-1970s, dealing mainly with an opiate-injecting clientele (Yates 1981). It is true that in the immediate aftermath of the removal of a general practitioner (GP)'s right to prescribe heroin or cocaine for addiction, many drug users outside London turned to other drugs, notably barbiturates and amphetamine. But this development was relatively short-lived and within a few years most had switched to a range of opioids including Palfium, pethidine and diconal; often continuing to use barbiturates as

---

6   The report *Drug Addiction: The Second Report of the Interdepartmental Committee* was universally known as 'The Second Brain Report' after the committee's chairman, Lord Brain.

a kind of safety-net much as today's heroin users use alcohol and/or temazepam/diazepam. This almost exclusive focus by the British drug treatment network meant that the two most widely used illicit drugs – amphetamine and cannabis – were paradoxically the two most widely ignored (Turner 1994).

Nikiforuk (1992) describes the impact throughout history of various plagues on the social, political and cultural life of the people. Since the Black Death swept across mediaeval Europe, the power of pestilence to change the way we think about, and act towards, our fellow citizens has been well recognized. The advent of the syphilis epidemic in Europe in 1493 with a small group of kidnapped Arawak Indians, on Christopher Columbus' return from the New World to Seville, changed the continent's sexual mores dramatically. The brief fashion for municipal bath-houses – really little more than municipal brothels without the financial element – disappeared with the arrival of the pox. Open-mouthed kissing disappeared so entirely in the UK that when it returned at the beginning of the twentieth century it was described as 'French kissing' (Nikiforuk 1992).

The arrival of acquired immune deficiency syndrome (AIDS) in the early 1980s was equally momentous. Little attention was paid to the development at first since it was seen as a disease affecting only American gays and African heterosexuals. However, with the discovery by Dr Roy Robertson, an Edinburgh GP (Robertson 1994), that significant numbers of his drug-using patients tested positive for human immunodeficiency virus (HIV) – the viral infection assumed to cause the condition known as AIDS – serious attention began to shift towards the drug-using community (Berridge 1996).

In the main this represented a self-protective reaction, since it was widely believed that drug users might form a 'bridgehead' between gays and the 'wider community'. In 1986 the McClelland Report – the result of a Scottish Office-appointed committee of enquiry into HIV positivity amongst the drug-using community in Edinburgh – concluded that in the circumstances, initiatives aimed at halting the spread of the disease were of more importance than preventing the increases in drug misuse (Scottish Office 1986). Two years later a ground-breaking report from the Advisory Council on the Misuse of Drugs (ACMD), *AIDS and Drug Misuse: Part I*, reached the same conclusion (ACMD 1988).

Almost overnight, agencies in the drugs field were encouraged to refocus their priorities to accommodate a shift towards more overt harm reduction initiatives. Drug services were encouraged to offer needle-exchange facilities. Funds were provided to allow community drug services to offer a substitute prescribing service (mainly methadone) for opioid injectors. As Berridge (1996) has pointed out, the ground had been prepared for this development for some time. An earlier ACMD report, *Treatment and Rehabilitation* (ACMD 1982), had argued for a shift away from traditional dependence/addiction models to the concept of the 'problem drug user'. Reducing the harm that drug users might do to themselves and, significantly, to those around them, became a legitimate goal. In some respects then, the changes which came about within the field were already beginning to happen *before* the advent of AIDS. Moreover, this came during a period when there had been a significant expansion in drug treatment services. Both agencies and the individuals within them were often new to the field.

Significantly, it was mainly those drug treatment services that had been established in the early 1970s which raised objections to the new direction which was now being taken. Those who had seen the silting up of the London clinics with heroin or Physeptone injectors, and the turning of counselling sessions into weekly arguments about dosage level, questioned the therapeutic efficacy of a return to substitute prescribing. Those ex-drug users – most of them within the voluntary sector – who had entered the field in order to help others to achieve abstinence, questioned the morality of prioritizing drug users who had no interest in 'coming off'. And this, they argued, would indeed be the effect of a return to more widespread prescribing. Under such a regime, inevitably, the ethos of abstinence would be undermined and those who would otherwise have considered abstinence would be drawn along with the flow and become 'geriatric junkies' neutered by substitute prescribing (Yates 1992).

As the AIDS epidemic has failed to materialize to anything like the extent which had been predicted in the mid 1980s, the focus has shifted towards the issues of crime prevention and community safety. The same approaches of substitute prescribing will, it is argued, make our city streets safer and reduce the incidence of burglary, car theft, shop-lifting etc. In addition, it is argued that by providing a licit, long-lasting opioid, the use not only of street heroin, but also of other associated drugs such as temazepam and Valium will decrease and thus impact upon the level of overdoses; particularly those resulting from the interaction of a cocktail of drugs. There is little evidence as yet, though, that a large-scale programme of substitute prescribing will indeed reduce overdosing in this way (McIntosh and McKeganey 2001).

The new recovery movement

The remedicalization of addiction treatment over the past two decades (McKeganey 2007) has effectively marginalized the recovery concept. Addiction treatment is overwhelmingly dominated by the NHS and many practitioners appear to have little interest or belief in recovery-oriented interventions (Best, Harris and Strang 2000). Substitute prescribing has become the treatment of choice, although, increasingly, there appears to be evidence that for significant numbers of clients this approach has failed to achieve the stated objective of eliminating the use of illicit substances (Best *et al.* 1999; Best *et al.* 2000; Best and Ridge 2003; Yates *et al.* 2005). Residential (recovery-oriented) treatment has become increasingly rare, reserved largely for those who have consistently failed to comply with community-based treatment plans (Yates 2008).

Not only are specialist addiction treatment staff sceptical of the merits of recovery; some appear to be actively resistant to recovery-oriented aspirations in their clients (Best, Harris and Strang 2000; Yates *et al.* 2005), with some arguing that recovery is not only naïve, but potentially dangerous (Ashton 2008). Increasingly, clients of drug treatment services are finding that if they wish to be abstinent then they will need to sustain this themselves (Noble *et al.* 2002).

However, a new recovery movement appears to be coalescing in the UK. As with the emergence of therapeutic communities for the treatment of addiction in the early 1970s (Broekaert *et al.* 2006; Yates 2003; Yates *et al.* 2006) these developments are largely non-medical and, often, fiercely anti-treatment. Many have adopted the 12-step framework pioneered by AA/Narcotics Anonymous (NA) fellowships but what is emerging is a far more robust and confrontational approach which vigorously challenges rationalization or dishonesty amongst fellow members and has, in many cases, discarded the spiritual ('higher power') elements of traditional AA/NA.

White (2007, 2008, 2009) and others have argued for a broader view of addiction and recovery; a view which is not simply focused upon the 'acute-care' model of treatment delivery but is widened to encompass the full trajectory of an individual's addiction and recovery. It has been recognized for some time that many, perhaps most, of those who become addicted may recover naturally (Vaillant 1983) and some have expressed concern that this natural remission might be undermined by certain treatment modalities (Winick 1962; Yates 1992). Understanding the motivation and aspirations of these emerging groups appears set to be the new challenge both for addiction treatment practitioners and researchers. Failure to respond to their demands risks alienating a growing community of drug users to the mainstream of addiction treatment.

References

Advisory Council on the Misuse of Drugs (ACMD) (1982) *Treatment and Rehabilitation.* London: HMSO.

Advisory Council on the Misuse of Drugs (ACMD) (1988) *AIDS & Drug Misuse: Part 1.* London: HMSO.

Armor, D., Polich, J. and Stambul, H. (1976) *Alcoholism and Treatment.* Santa Monica, CA: Rand Corp. Publications (R 1739).

Arthur, T.S. (1843) *Temperance Tales or Six Nights with the Washingtonians.* Philadelphia, PA: Godey and M'Michael.

Ashton, M. (2008) 'The new abstentionists.' *Druglink* (Special Insert), Dec/Jan 2008.

Bamber, S. and Best, D. (2009) 'Recovery as the art of life itself: The Recovery Form bulletin.' *Addiction Today,* September/October, 28–29.

Basler, R.P. (1953) (ed.) *The Collected Works of Abraham Lincoln.* New Brunswick, NJ: Rutgers University Press.

Berridge, V. (1996) *AIDS in the U.K.: The Making of Policy 1981–1994.* Oxford: Oxford University Press.

Best, D., Gossop, M., Stewart, D., Marsden, J., Lehmann, P. and Strang, J. (1999) 'Continued heroin use during methadone treatment: Relationships between frequency of use and reasons reported for heroin use.' *Drug and Alcohol Dependence 53,* 191–195.

Best, D., Harris, J., Gossop, M., Farrell, M., Finch, E., Noble, A. and Strang, J. (2000) 'Use of non-prescribed methadone and other illicit drugs during methadone maintenance treatment.' *Drug and Alcohol Review 19,* 9–16.

Best, D., Harris, J. and Strang, J. (2000) 'The NHS AA/NA: NHS attitudes to 12 step help.' *Addiction Today 11,* 65, 17–19.

Best, D. and Ridge, G. (2003) 'Using on Top and the Problems It Brings: Additional Drug Use by Methadone Treatment Patients.' In G. Tober and J. Strang (eds) *Methadone Matters: Evolving Community Methadone Treatment of Opiate Addiction.* London: Martin Dunitz.

Betty Ford Institute Consensus Panel (2007) 'What is recovery? A working definition from the Betty Ford Institute.' *Journal of Substance Abuse Treatment 33,* 221–228.

Blocker, J., Fahey, D. and Tyrrell, I. (2003) *Alcohol and Temperance in Modern History: An International Encyclopedia.* Santa Barbara, CA: ABC-CLIO Ltd.

Bonner, A. (1990) *Jerry McAuley and his Mission.* New York: Loizeaux Brothers.

Broekaert, E., Vandervelde, S., Soyez, V., Yates, R. and Slater, A. (2006) 'The Third Generation of Therapeutic Communities: The early development of the TCs for addiction in Europe.' *European Addiction Research 12,* 2–11.

Clayson, A. (1995) *Beat Merchants: The Origins, Impact and Rock Legacy of the 1960's British Pop Groups.* London: Blandford.

Davies, D.L. (1962) 'Normal drinking in recovered alcohol addicts.' *Quarterly Journal of Studies on Alcohol 23,* 94–104.

Day, E., Gaston, R., Furlong, E., Murali, V. and Coppello, A. (2005) 'United Kingdom substance misuse treatment workers' attitudes toward 12-step self-help groups.' *Journal of Substance Abuse Treatment 29,* 321–327.

Dubiel, R. (2004) *The Road to Fellowship: The Role of the Emmanuel Movement and the Jacoby Club in the Development of Alcoholics Anonymous.* New York: iUniverse Inc.

Glatt, M. (1952) 'Drinking habits of English middle-class alcoholics.' *Acta Psychiatrica Scandinavica 37*, 88–113.

Gusfield, J.R. (1963) *Symbolic Crusade: Status Politics and the American Temperance Movement.* Urbana, IL: University of Illinois Press.

Herring, J.B. (1877) *Kenekuk, the Kickapoo Prophet.* Lawrence, KS: University of Kansas Press.

Hingson, R., Scotch, N. and Goldman, E. (1977) 'Impact of the Rand Report on alcoholics, treatment personnel and Boston residents.' *Journal of Studies on Alcohol 38*, 2065–2076.

HM Government (1965) *Drug Addiction: The Second Report of the Interdepartmental Committee.* London: HMSO.

HM Government (2008) *Drugs: Protecting Families and Communities: The 2008 Drug Strategy.* London: HMSO.

Inglis, B. (1975) *The Forbidden Game: A Social History of Drugs.* London: Hodder & Stoughton.

Jellinek, E. (1952) 'Phases of alcohol addiction.' *Quarterly Journal of Studies on Alcohol 13*, 673.

Jellinek, E. (1960) *The Disease Concept of Alcoholism.* New Haven, CT: Hillhouse Press.

Keller, M. (1962) 'The Definition of Alcoholism and the Estimation of Its Prevalence.' In D. Pittman and C. Snyder (eds) *Society, Culture and Drinking Patterns.* New York and London: Wiley.

King, E. (1979) *Scotland Sober and Free: The Temperance Movement, 1829–1979.* Glasgow: Glasgow Museums and Art Galleries.

Kohn, M. (1992) *Dope Girls: The Birth of the British Underground.* London: Lawrence & Wishart.

Levine, H. (1978) 'The discovery of addiction: Changing conceptions of habitual drunkenness in America.' *Journal of Studies on Alcohol 39*, 143–174.

Levine, H. (1984) 'The alcohol problem in America: From temperance to alcoholism.' *British Journal of Addiction 79*, 109–119.

Longmate, N. (1968) *The Waterdrinkers: A History of Temperance.* London: Hamish Hamilton.

McCarthy, K. (1984) 'Early alcoholism treatment: The Emmanuel Movement and Richard Peabody.' *Journal of Studies on Alcohol 45*, 59–74.

McCormick, M. (1969) 'First representations of the gamma alcoholic in the English novel.' *Quarterly Journal of Studies on Alcohol 30*, 957–980.

McIntosh, J. and McKeganey, N. (2001) *Beating the Dragon: Recovery from Dependent Drug Use.* London: Pearson Education.

McKeganey, N. (2007) 'The challenge to UK drug policy.' *Drugs: Education, Prevention and Policy 14*, 559–571.

McLaughlin, P. (1989) 'Responding to drunkenness in Scottish society: A socio-historical study of responses to alcohol problems.' PhD thesis, University of Stirling.

McLaughlin, P. (1991) 'Inebriate Reformatories in Scotland: An Institutional History.' In S. Barrows and R. Room (eds) *Drinking: Behavior and Belief in Modern History.* Berkeley, CA: University of California Press.

MacLeod, R.M. (1967) 'The edge of hope: Social policy and chronic alcoholism 1870–1900.' *Journal of the History of Medicine 23*, 215–245.

Maxwell, M. (1950) 'The Washingtonian movement.' *Quarterly Journal of Studies on Alcohol 11*, 410–451.

Mitcheson, M. (1994) 'Drug Clinics in the 1970s.' In J. Strang and M. Gossop (eds) *Heroin Addiction and Drug Policy: The British System.* Oxford: Oxford University Press.

Nikiforuk, A. (1992) *The Fourth Horseman: A Short History of Epidemics, Plagues and Other Scourges.* London: Fourth Estate.

Noble, A., Best, D., Man, L.H., Gossop, M. and Strang, J. (2002) 'Self-detoxification attempts among methadone maintenance patients: What methods and what success?' *Addictive Behaviors 27*, 575–584.

Offord, R.M. (1970) *Jerry McAuley: An Apostle to the Lost*, 7th edn. New York: Books for Libraries Press.

Parker, A.C. (1913) *The Code of Handsome Lake, the Seneca Prophet*. Charleston, SC: Forgotten Books.

Paterson, A. (1969) *The Golden Years of the Clyde Steamers*. Newton Abbot: David & Charles.

Peele, S. (1995) *The Diseasing of America*. New York: Lexington Books.

Rawlings, B. and Yates, R. (2001) 'Fallen Angel: An Introduction.' In B. Rawlings and R. Yates (eds) *Therapeutic Communities for the Treatment of Drug Users*. London: Jessica Kingsley Publishers.

Robertson, R. (1994) 'The Arrival of HIV.' In J. Strang and M. Gossop (eds) *Heroin Addiction and Drug Policy: The British System*. Oxford: Oxford University Press.

Roizen, R. (1987) 'The Great Controlled-Drinking Controversy.' In M. Galanter (ed.) *Recent Developments in Alcoholism*, vol. 5. New York: Plenum Press.

Room, R. (1983) 'Sociological Aspects of the Disease Concept of Alcoholism.' In R. Smart, F. Glaser and Y. Israel (eds) *Alcohol and Drug Problems*, vol. 7. New York and London: Plenum.

Room, R. (2001) 'Intoxication and bad behaviour: understanding cultural differences in the link.' *Social Science and Medicine 53*, 189–198.

Room, R. (2003) 'The cultural framing of addiction.' *Janus Head 6*, 221–234.

Scottish Government (2008) *The Road to Recovery: A New Approach to Tackling Scotland's Drug Problem*. Edinburgh: Scottish Government.

Scottish Office (1986) *Report of the Scottish Committee on HIV (AIDS) Infection and Drug Misuse*. Edinburgh: HMSO.

Shapiro, H. (1988) *Waiting for the Man*. London: Mandarin Press.

Shapiro, H. (2005) *Shooting Stars: Drugs, Hollywood and the Movies*. London: Serpent's Tail.

Smith, D.G. (1985) 'Handsome Lake Religion.' In *Canadian Encyclopaedia*, vol. II. Toronto: Historica Foundation.

Spear, H.B. (1994) 'The Early Years of Britain's Drug Situation in Practice: Up to the 1960s.' In J. Strang and M. Gossop (eds) *Heroin Addiction and Drug Policy: The British System*, vol. 1. *Origins and Evolution*. Oxford: Oxford University Press.

Spear, H.B. (2002) *Heroin Addiction Care and Control: The British System 1916–1984* (edited by Joy Mott). London: DrugScope.

Sturtevant, W. and Trigger, B. (1978) *Handbook of North American Indians: Northeast*, vol. 15. Washington, DC: Smithsonian Institute.

Trice, H. and Wahl, J. (1958) 'A rank order analysis of the symptoms of alcoholism.' *Quarterly Journal of Studies on Alcohol 19*, 636–640.

Turner, D. (1994) 'The Development of the Voluntary Sector, No Further Need for Pioneers?' In J. Strang and M. Gossop (eds) *Heroin Addiction and Drug Policy: The British System*. Oxford: Oxford University Press.

Vaillant, G.E. (1983) *Natural History of Alcoholism*. Cambridge, MA: Harvard University Press.

White, W. (2000) 'The history of recovered people as wounded healers: From Native America to the rise of the modern alcoholism movement.' *Alcoholism Treatment Quarterly 18*, 1–23.

White, W. (2001) 'Pre-A.A. alcoholic mutual aid societies.' *Alcoholism Treatment Quarterly 19*, 1–21.

White, W. (2007) 'Addiction recovery: Its definition and conceptual boundaries.' *Journal of Substance Abuse Treatment 33*, 229–241.

White, W. (2008) *Recovery Management and Recovery-Oriented Systems of Care: Scientific Rationale and Promising Practices*. Philadelphia, PA: North East Addiction Technology Transfer Centre/ Great Lakes Addiction Technology Transfer Centre/Philadelphia Department of Behavioral Health & Mental Retardation Services.

White, W. (2009) *Peer Based Addiction Recovery Support: History, Theory, Practice and Scientific Evaluation*. Philadelphia, PA: Great Lakes Addiction Technology Transfer Centre/ Philadelphia Department of Behavioral Health & Mental Retardation Services.

White, W. and Whiters, D. (2005) 'Faith-based recovery: Its historical roots.' *Counselor 6*, 58–62.

Winick, C. (1962) 'Maturing out of narcotic addiction.' *United Nations Bulletin on Narcotics 14*, 1–7.

World Health Organization (1992) *The ICD-10 Classification of Mental and Behavioural Disorders: Clinical Descriptions and Diagnostic Guidelines.* Geneva: World Health Organization.

Yates, R. (1981) *Out from the Shadows.* London: NACRO.

Yates, R. (1992) *If It Weren't for the Alligators – A History of Drugs, Music & Popular Culture in Manchester.* Manchester: Lifeline Project.

Yates, R. (1999a) *Only Available in Black: The Limiting of Addiction Services in the Twentieth Century.* Uteseksjonen 30 Ar Pa Gata. Oslo: Uteseksjonen.

Yates, R. (1999b) *Shoot Out the Lights: The Failure of Objective Reason to Frame the Response to Drug Realities.* Uteseksjonen 30 Ar Pa Gata. Oslo: Uteseksjonen.

Yates, R. (2002) 'A brief history of British drug policy, 1950–2001.' *Drugs, Education, Prevention and Policy 9*, 113–124.

Yates, R. (2003) 'A brief moment of glory: The impact of the therapeutic community movement on drug treatment systems in the UK.' *International Journal of Social Welfare 12*, 239–243.

Yates, R. (2008) 'Different strokes for different folks: Results of a small study comparing characteristics of a therapeutic community population with a community drug project population.' *International Journal of Therapeutic Communities 29*, 44–56.

Yates, R. and McIvor, G. (2003) 'Alcohol and the Criminal Justice System in Scotland.' In S. Kilcommins and I. O'Donnell (eds) *Alcohol, Society and Law.* Chichester: Barry Rose Law Publishers.

Yates, R., McIvor, G., Eley, S., Malloch, M. and Barnsdale, L. (2005) 'Coercion in Drug Treatment: The Impact on Motivation, Aspiration and Outcome.' In M. Pedersen, V. Segraeus and M. Hellman (eds) *Evidence Based Practice – Challenges in Substance Abuse Treatment: Proceedings of the 7th International Symposium on Substance Treatment, November 25–27, 2004, Aarhus.* Helsinki: Nordic Council for Alcohol and Drug Research/University of Aarhus/EWODOR/EFTC.

Yates, R., Rawlings, B., Broekaert, E. and De Leon, G. (2006) 'Brief encounters: The development of European drug-free therapeutic communities and the origins of the European Federation of Therapeutic Communities.' *International Journal of Therapeutic Communities 27*, 5–11.

CHAPTER 2

Mapping Routes to Recovery: The Role of Recovery Groups and Communities

David Best

Background

The advent of a recovery agenda has been characterized by the translation of an international definition of recovery (Betty Ford Institute Consensus Group 2007) into local plans for action (e.g. Scottish Government 2008), with an increased thrust and emphasis around helping drug (and alcohol) addicts to turn their lives around and to make substantial positive changes in their lives. Yet our knowledge of recovery is extremely limited in research terms, relying rather on the anecdotal stories of those in recovery and on an evidence base for 12-step and other mutual aid that is largely North American (Humphreys 2004) and about which there is some scepticism among professionals in the UK. The aim of this chapter is to make a number of observations about what is the current state of drug treatment in England and to demonstrate the challenges faced by a recovery movement in terms of what treatment means for most people in the UK. Our attention then turns to some preliminary findings about recovery from UK samples that not only confirm that recovery is possible for many people but may also offer some insights into what we are asking of people in their attempts to overcome addiction problems.

Researching methadone treatment

> Addiction is not self-curing. Left alone, addiction only gets worse, leading to total degradation, to prison, and ultimately to death. (Robert Dupont, Director of NIDA, 2007, pp.xi–xii)

> As with treatments for these other chronic medical conditions [hypertension, diabetes, asthma], there is no cure for addiction. (O'Brien and McLellan, *The Lancet*, 1996, p.240)

We have generated a model of addiction, especially drug addiction, that is extremely pessimistic, in part because our goals and expectations for this form of treatment are so low. Two mantras predominate: 'addiction is a chronic, relapsing condition' and the aim of harm reduction maintenance treatment is to 'keep people alive and out of jail'. As a consequence, our studies of methadone treatment start with low expectations and can afford a critical approach because our perspective of the client group and their long-term prognosis is pessimistic.

The first paper I was involved in at the National Addiction Centre (NAC) – 'Time of day of methadone consumption and illicit heroin use: A study in two South London drug clinics' (Best *et al.* 1997) – was about clients timing their trips to the clinic for on-site dispensing to allow them to use heroin. Thus, the two dominant patterns in this group were early morning on-site methadone consumption to enable heroin use in the evening, often alongside other drugs, or late collection of methadone to allow heroin use in the late morning or early afternoon. In other words, it was assumed that the use of methadone would not be enough for many clients who would manipulate the daily on-site dispensing routine by using the flexible opening hours to 'use on top'. This is consistent with an oppositional model in which staff and clients are engaged in a 'game' of boundary testing and control.

The next year, I was involved in a second paper 'Eating too little, smoking and drinking too much: Wider lifestyle problems among methadone maintenance patients' (Best *et al.* 1998), which addressed issues familiar to critics of the 'social control' perspective of methadone. In this paper we identified a considerable proportion of clients who were daily, dependent drinkers, who had a lifestyle that revolved around the clinic. The notion of 'methadone, wine and welfare' is not a new one but this was a paper that was written from within one of the main prescribing centres in England and whose authorship included a psychiatrist who had championed methadone maintenance prescribing. The reason why this is possible is that it occurs within a model where expectations are so low that a certain amount of collateral damage is acceptable. It was, however, written before the advent of the crime reduction agenda in UK drug policy, although its message – that there can be public health and safety gains while the individuals show no sign of 'getting better' – has considerable relevance to the current debate about 'who benefits' from treatment.

Methadone is not the only fruit?

I then moved to Birmingham where I became involved in rolling out an initiative from the National Treatment Agency for Substance Misuse called the Treatment Effectiveness Initiative (National Treatment Agency for Substance Misuse 2005). The aim of this process was to improve the quality of delivery of psychosocial interventions in drug treatment and, to prepare for this initiative, Birmingham conducted an audit of all specialist adult drug treatment services to assess what typically occurs in treatment sessions. Our findings (reported in Best *et al.* in press) were not encouraging – the majority of clients were seen fortnightly and were typically seen for around 45 minutes in each session. In other words, the total contact time per client is around 90 minutes per month, or 18 hours a year if the treatment lasts that long. However, it was our analysis of what that time consists of that is the greatest cause for concern, as shown in Figure 2.1.

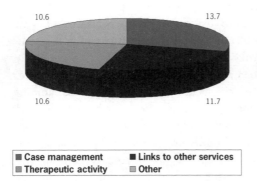

Therapeutic activity	% of clients ever discussed	% discussed in last session
Complementary therapies	10.5%	3.2%
Alcohol treatment	9.3%	4.4%
Harm reduction	68.3%	29.4%
Motivational enhancement	1.5%	1.2%
Relapse prevention	66.3%	34.0%
Other structured interventions	22.7%	14.0%
Care planning	78.8%	21.2%

■ Case management　■ Links to other services
■ Therapeutic activity　▨ Other

Figure 2.1 Time spent (in minutes) in last drug working session

In the average session, the initial activities that were typically undertaken were case management activities around prescription management, drug testing and results, compliance and signposting. There was very little time available for, or commitment to, delivering evidence-based psychosocial interventions. In other words, what is called treatment, for the majority of clients on substitute prescribing is, in fact, 'a script and a chat'. When we looked in more detail at what goes on in one of the criminal justice teams (Best *et al.* 2009), what we found was that workers are caught between the role of case managers and the role of therapists, and that it is the therapeutic identity that becomes secondary at times of considerable demands around risk management and clinical governance.

We have since repeated this work in a second partnership area in the West Midlands of England. Here we found that the average contact time in drug and alcohol services run by the NHS was 63 minutes per month. In this review of 753 clients currently engaged in treatment, clients averaged 5.4 contacts in the last three months, and the average session lasted 34.5 minutes. The service consisted of three teams with the average contact times among the drug teams being:

- community drug team – 69 minutes
- criminal justice team – 68 minutes
- shared care team – 48 minutes.

So not only was there low level of contact, this also did not seem to be differentiated by where the client was in their 'treatment journey'. This is prescribing and not treatment and, in effect, the prescription 'swamps' all of the other elements of the treatment process.

The problem is that this arises from the exceptionally low expectations that services have of outcomes. Most clients get caught in this model of safety first prescribing without end, and the 'therapeutic' part of the treatment is generally delivered by workers who do not believe that meaningful recovery is possible. This generates a vicious circle where clients are not encouraged to and so do not pursue lasting change.

A brief diversion – developmental models in criminology

In 2004 John H. Laub and Robert J. Sampson published a book entitled *Shared Beginnings, Divergent Lives: Delinquent Boys to Age 70*, which is based on interviews with a cohort of 70-year-old men who had been remanded to reform school in Boston in the 1940s. The key methodological approach is to take a 'life-course' or developmental perspective to assessing offending careers. There are three main conclusions that derive from this work:

1. The vast majority of offenders 'mature out' of offending.

2. The 'risk factors' that appear so potent in early years – poverty, poor schooling, early onset of substance use and offending, and so on – have little predictive power in mapping long-term offending trajectories.

3. The two key predictors of long-term desistance from offending are getting a job the person is happy with and being in a relationship (with partner or whole family) that the person is comfortable with. 'Treatment' or interventions were not strong predictors of positive outcomes.

Why is this relevant to a book about recovery from addiction problems? It is only an analogy – not all drug users are offenders and not all offenders are drug users, but nonetheless there are important lessons to learn. The first of these lessons is that we need to take a longer perspective if we want to understand whether people will 'grow out' of addiction problems and, to continue the parallel, most, but not all, will. The second point is that what will enable people to grow out of their addiction problems are to do with broader life issues not to do with short-term interventions. Thus, the implication is that, regardless of what 'treatment' can offer, it is a wider social movement towards building 'social capital' that is important in supporting people to sustain recovery journeys.

For Laub and Sampson (2004) the key 'desistance predictors' are:

- attachment to a conventional person (spouse)

- stable employment

- transformation of personal identity

- ageing

- interpersonal skills

- life and coping skills.

Although we cannot assume the equivalence for substance users, we do relatively little to support or enable those factors, particularly given the findings of the UK studies reported above indicating what drug treatment means in practice for many people. This will also be reflected in the recovery research findings below about what our current evidence base suggests.

The notion of recovery as linked to social capital is also important in two senses. There is the traditional view of social capital as 'The sum of the resources, actual or virtual, that accrue to an individual or a group by virtue of possessing a durable network of more or less institutionalised relationships of mutual acquaintance and recognition' (Bourdieu 1975). However, there is also a second sense much more akin to a Hobbesian social contract in which social capital also manifests as the extent of the individual's commitment to social norms and processes. In other words, it is both an issue about the support systems that an individual has and about their desire to commit to conventional values around families, jobs and aspirations. Thus, within the model developed by Laub and Sampson, this may well involve maturational processes including ageing and a transformation of personal identity.

The evidence for recovery

Much of our understanding of recovery comes from two sources: studies of natural recovery and treatment outcome studies. To consider the natural recovery model first, it is important to bear in mind that for many substances and in many settings this is the norm, and the notion of institutionalized treatment as a necessary component of recovery is alien. Perhaps the most obvious example of this is smoking, but Sobell, Cunningham and Sobell (1996) reported rates of 75% and 77% recovery without formal help in drinkers in remission. Cunningham (2000) assessed recovery from a range of substances, and reported that the use of any formal treatment ranged from 43.1% for cannabis to 90.7% for heroin, with 59.7% of cocaine users seeking formal treatment at some point in their recovery journeys. In other words, for many people the way that they have achieved recovery is through their own volition and with strategies that do not necessitate formal treatment interventions.

Granfield and Cloud (2001) have suggested that 'Those who possess larger amounts of social capital, perhaps even independently of the intensity of use, will be likely candidates for less intrusive forms of treatment' (Granfield and Cloud 2001, p.1550), within this model that suggests that treatment is a slightly unusual way of addressing addiction problems and one that may be adopted by only a small (and not particularly representative) group of people who get into trouble with alcohol or drugs.

Even within the treatment population, however, the evidence for positive outcomes for intensive, abstinence-oriented interventions is reasonably good. Gossop *et al.* (2002), reporting on the two-year outcomes from the English National Treatment Outcome Research Study (NTORS), found that 48% of admissions to residential treatment were abstinent from all opiates two years after admission, with the majority of this group sustaining abstinence over the period of two years. While the abstinence rates were lower in the Scottish treatment outcome study (DORIS: McKeganey *et al.* 2006), a similar conclusion was reached – if abstinence is the goal, then residential treatments are more likely to support this objective. From a developmental or careers model, this is not surprising. For a shift in a trajectory of drug use to be sustained, there is likely to have to be a 'turning point' (Hser, Longshore and Anglin 2007) that enables broad lifestyle change and does not simply address the immediate profile of physical symptoms.

The US recovery movement

There are two important recovery movements that have emerged in the US specific to substance use. Recovery-oriented integrated systems (ROIS: De Leon 2007) have emerged out of the therapeutic community movement and are described elsewhere in this book (Chapters 5 and 6). The second has been led by the phenomenal work of William White and his collaborators and colleagues and will be the focus of this section of the chapter. What this movement has done is to offer both hope and direction to the addictions field – a hope that is now tangible in the UK and, while it is being grasped by policy makers, is a hope that is springing from a ground level, and is apparent in recovery communities across the UK.

In 2008 Alexandre Laudet summed this view up in an editorial in which she concluded that 'Understanding recovery and identifying factors that promote or hinder it will require a number of paradigm shifts for addiction professionals, including moving from an acute care model to a chronic or long-term approach, and shifting the focus of research and service provision from symptoms to wellness' (Laudet 2008, p.1681). The inspiration of this model is to look to success and to celebrate and build on those who have done it and to utilize them as the key 'recovery capital' resources in both developing our understanding of addiction issues and in providing the right kinds of support. William White has claimed that:

> Recovery involves three critical elements: 1) sobriety (abstinence from alcohol drugs and unprescribed drugs), 2) improvement in global health (physical, emotional, relational and ontological – life meaning and purpose) and 3) citizenship (positive participation in and contribution to community life). (White 2009, p.16)

White has gone on to argue that a recovery model has a number of key features – that there is a recovery orientation rather than simply stabilization, that the model is strengths based in that it focuses on individual strengths and on recovery capital rather than disease and disability, that recovery is more interpersonal than intra-personal, and that it is based on a set of core skills. These include the planning of recovery, linking natural and formal recovery support systems and the development of personal and family resources. The focus is on the present and the future not on causes or past experiences.

The core conclusions of this model are not that there is no place for what we have thought of as treatment, but its place is early in the treatment journey where the focus is rightly on the physical well-being and symptom management components of recovery. What the recovery movement has taught us is that, while necessary, these are not sufficient and that recovery is much more socially located and embedded in a broader agenda of growth and development for individuals but also for their families and their communities.

The emerging evidence base for recovery in the UK

Our starting point for this research work was simple – I was struck that we knew so little about what factors allowed those who made it to abstinence to sustain it, and, consequently, at a service commissioning and a service delivery level, we offered so little support to those who reached this point (this early point) in their recovery journeys.

The initial steps of this programme of work have been stumbling and are beset with methodological issues and problems, that reflect the nature of what we are trying to do. The initial investigation involved distributing a simple, four-page questionnaire at a conference held in London largely attended by people in recovery. We then extended this by distributing the questionnaire at the reunion of a rehab unit in Scotland (Castle Craig) and including copies in the middle of a magazine. In traditional research methods terms, this is a sampling disaster and generates all kinds of questions of representativeness but something arose out of this work that was much more encouraging. The short questionnaire was basically anonymous, although a box was included asking people if they would be willing to contribute to follow-ups. The response to this was incredible – more than three-quarters of those who filled in the questionnaire provided details and, just as crucially, acted as advocates and sponsors of the project, getting friends to fill it in.

So what did we find? The first slice of the data (Best *et al.* 2008) focused on 107 former heroin users, the majority of whom were working in the addictions field at the time of the study. They were predominantly male and white, and they had been working for around seven years at the time of the study. When asked what enabled them to finally give up using heroin, the answer was most commonly about 'having had enough', a gradual process of not wanting to live that life any more, but also involving an event – family or health related in many cases – that finally gave them the impetus to make the initial change. However, the key finding from our study was that participants readily differentiated between the factors that allowed them to achieve abstinence and the factors that allowed them to sustain it. The most important factors in sustaining recovery were 'moving away from substance-using friends', suitable accommodation and support from non-using friends. In other words, it was the development of a support network that allowed recovery to be sustained. The findings also suggested that engagement with Narcotics Anonymous (NA) was a common feature in many of the recovery journeys reported.

This cohort study has continued to grow and a second paper has now been published (Best *et al.* 2009) based on a larger cohort of 269 former heroin users and drinkers, based on three groups: primary drinkers (n=98), primary heroin users (n=104) and those who reported problems with both alcohol and drugs (n=67). Former heroin users reported more rapid escalation to problematic use but much shorter careers involving daily use than was the case in the alcohol cohort. Alcohol and heroin users also differed in their self-reported reasons for stopping use, with drinkers more likely to report work and social reasons and drug users to report criminal justice factors. In sustaining abstinence, alcohol users more often reported partner support and drug users peer support, and former drug users were also more likely to emphasize the need to move away from substance-using friends than was the case for former drinkers. Users of both alcohol and heroin were least likely to cite partner factors in sustaining recovery, but were more likely to need to move away from using friends and then to cite reasonable accommodation as crucial in sustaining abstinence.

There are two implications here. The first is that it is further evidence of what little knowledge we have of recovery pathways and how they may vary. The evidence from the study is that different substance profiles may have different implications for recovery pathways and routes – and also for the likelihood that people will use either mutual aid groups or formal treatment services – but says little about what the effect of location, gender, ethnicity, age and other such factors might be on recovery pathways. It also says little about non-abstinent recovery. However, the key discovery was not a finding, but about the conduct of the study, that it was a positive experience for both researchers and the participants and the sense that conducting recovery research was filling a real gap that made it feel much more like action research and participation.

This has inspired the current programme of research currently being rolled out in Birmingham and Glasgow, which has three aims:

1. to map out the support groups in each setting that support alcohol and heroin recovery journeys

2. to collate the experiences of recovery of people at different stages of the recovery journeys and their support needs at different stages

3. to assess the role that different interventions play in supporting recovery pathways at different stages of recovery journeys.

Although it is too early to present many results for the study, there are some key points to make. The Birmingham study had a target of 100 drug users in recovery, and the method involved use of peer interviewers and no researchers. At the time of writing the sample stands at 141, the majority of whom (around three-quarters) have expressed interest in either becoming recovery coaches or advocates and/or in being trained to be peer research interviewers. The aim of both projects is also to assess the relationship between maintained and abstinent recovery. Similarly, in Glasgow, there has been enormous support for the project and again it will run on peer lines with users in recovery acting as the researchers and some taking on a more active role in the study management and development. As William White has argued, this is not traditional clinical research because the act of participating can be a part of the recovery journey and the research process is participative and celebratory. This work will shed light on some 'hypotheses' about recovery pathways but its significance is much more likely to revolve around its charting of the optimism and drive that characterizes recovery communities in the UK.

So where does this leave us?

The recovery agenda creates a massive agenda for researchers. We not only need to do the basic work of mapping out pathways to recovery and developing 'developmental' models of addiction and recovery, we also need to couch this in a new language and in a new series of research methods. Our experience to date has been that there is a huge appetite among people in recovery not only to take part in this kind of research but to have a stake in it and to own the results. For this reason, we cannot pretend to dispassionate observer status and we have to find academically credible ways of developing quantitative as well as qualitative approaches to action research that is owned by people in recovery. There is an increasing recognition in the UK that people do recover but we have little to say about how or when at the moment, and almost nothing to tell policy makers about what they can do (and what treatment services can do to help). We are riding on a wave of enthusiasm and optimism at present – it is essential that this is translated into meaningful change and evidence.

References

Best, D., Day, E., Morgan, B., Oza, T., Copello, A. and Gossop, M. 'What treatment means in practice: An analysis of the therapeutic activity provided in criminal justice drug treatment services in Birmingham, England.' *Addiction Research and Theory* (in press).

Best, D., Ghufran, S., Day, E., Ray, R. and Loaring, J. (2008) 'Breaking the habit: A retrospective analysis of desistance factors among formerly problematic heroin users.' *Drug and Alcohol Review 27*, 619–624.

Best, D.W., Gossop, M., Marsden, J., Farrell, M. and Strang, J. (1997) 'Time of day of methadone consumption and illicit heroin use: A study in two South London drug clinics.' *Drug and Alcohol Dependence 49*, 49–54.

Best, D., Lehmann, P., Gossop, M., Harris, J., Noble, J. and Strang, J. (1998) 'Eating too little, smoking and drinking too much: Wider lifestyle problems among methadone maintenance patients.' *Addiction Research 6*, 489–498.

Best, D., Wood, K., Sweeting, R., Morgan, B. and Day, E. (2009) 'Fitting a quart into a black box: Keyworking in quasi-coercive drug treatment in England.' *Drugs: Education, Prevention and Policy 16*, 6, 1–18.

Betty Ford Institute Consensus Group (2007) 'What is recovery? A working definition from the Betty Ford Institute.' *Substance Abuse Treatment 33*, 221–228.

Bourdieu, P. (1975) 'The specificity of the scientific field and the social conditions of the progress of reason.' *Social Science Information 14*, 19–47.

Cunningham, J. (2000) 'Remissions from drug dependence: Is treatment a prerequisite?' *Drug and Alcohol Dependence 59*, 211–213.

De Leon, G. (2007) 'Toward a recovery oriented integrated system.' *Offender Substance Abuse Report 11*, 6, 81–88.

Dupont, R. (2007) 'Addiction in medicine.' *Transactions of the American Clinical and Climatological Association*, 13 November 2007.

Gossop, M., Marsden, J., Stewart, D. and Treacy, S. (2002) 'Change and stability of change after treatment of drug misuse: 2-year outcomes from the National Treatment Outcome Research Study (UK).' *Addictive Behaviours 27*, 155–166.

Granfield, R. and Cloud, W. (2001) 'Social context and "natural recovery": The role of social capital in the resolution of drug-associated problems.' *Substance Use and Misuse 36*, 11, 1543–1570.

Hser, Y., Longshore, D. and Anglin, M.D. (2007) 'The life course perspective on drug use: A conceptual framework for understanding drug use trajectories.' *Evaluation Review 31*, 515–547.

Humphreys, K. (2004) *Circles of Recovery: Self-help Organisations for Addictions.* Cambridge: Cambridge University Press.

Laub, J.H. and Sampson, R.J. (2004) *Shared Beginnings, Divergent Lives: Delinquent Boys to Age 70.* Cambridge, MA: Harvard University Press.

Laudet, A. (2008) 'Editorial: Recovery is life.' *Substance Use and Misuse 43*, 12, 1681–1684.

McKeganey, N., Bloor, M., Robertson, M., Neale, J. and MacDougall, J. (2006) 'Abstinence and drug abuse treatment: Results from the Drug Outcome Research in Scotland study.' *Drugs: Education, Prevention and Policy 13*, 537–550.

National Treatment Agency for Substance Misuse (2005) *Treatment Effectiveness Strategy.* NTA Business Plan 2005. London: National Treatment Agency.

O'Brien, C.P. and McLellan, A.T. (1996) 'Myths about the treatment of addiction.' *Lancet 347*, 237–240.

Scottish Government (2008) *The Road to Recovery: A New Approach to Tackling Scotland's Drug Problem.* Edinburgh: Scottish Government.

Sobell, L., Cunningham, J. and Sobell, M. (1996) 'Recovery from alcohol problems with and without treatment: Prevalence in two population surveys.' *American Journal of Public Health 86*, 966–972.

White, W. (2009) *Peer Based Addiction Recovery Support: History, Theory, Practice and Scientific Evaluation.* Philadelphia, PA: North East Addiction Technology Transfer Centre/Great Lakes Addiction Technology Transfer Centre/Philadelphia Department of Behavioral Health & Mental Retardation Services.

CHAPTER 3

Recovery in the Project: A South East Alternatives Journey

Dharmacarini Kuladharini

Turning Point Scotland (TPS)'s newly appointed recovery impact worker, Eric, opened the door to the project and was met by a slightly cross service manager. A startled Eric thrust a copy of a recovery resource pack at her saying, 'This will get you started on the road to recovery.'

'Really?' came the distracted reply. 'We might get to that after we've carried out the hundred and one other tasks on our existing project plan,' and with that she shut the door politely but firmly in his face. Later that day she absent-mindedly leafed through the recovery resource pack discarding much that seemed to be no novelty to a community rehabilitation project. Her eye was caught, however, by a simple recovery definition offered by the Scottish Recovery Network. 'Wow – that's it!' she thought. It was the answer to a question she didn't know she had been asking.

> Recovery is being able to live a meaningful and satisfying life, as defined by each person, in the presence or absence of symptoms. It is about having control over and input into one's own life. Each individual's recovery, like his or her experience of mental health problems or illness is a unique and deeply personal process. It is important to be clear that there is no right or wrong way to recover. (Scottish Recovery Network 2009)

South East Alternatives (SEA) was the first of six community rehabilitation services to be purchased by Glasgow Addiction Service (GAS). SEA's task was to provide structured day programmes for adults with alcohol or drug misuse problems in the south east area of Glasgow.

Managed by Turning Point Scotland, South East Alternatives opened its doors in 2001. By 2007, however, the service was in trouble. Concerns about SEA's service delivery performance were being expressed by purchasers, the Care Commission, the staff themselves and local Community Addiction Teams (CAT). There were apparently 60 people on programme but there was no clarity around what that actually meant or when the work was complete. Only a small proportion of those on programme actually attended groups. The staff were working with shoddy equipment, poorly laid out premises and no manager. The Care Commission in its 2006 inspection classified the project 'Medium Risk' and the purchasers had insisted on a full project plan to address the backlog of quality, resource and data issues at the project. Referrals from local CATs were at an all time low.

Turning Point Scotland took the first steps towards resolving these difficulties by separating SEA from its sister service Milestone and appointing a dedicated manager in each service. On 1 May 2007 the author, Dharmacarini Kuladharini,[1] at SEA and Kim Ross at Milestone took up post as service managers. It would be unfair to say that the prognosis for the service was entirely bleak. The service had been well respected and thriving at various times in its lifecycle. On the asset side, the current team were dedicated group workers and strong advocates for change. They had been delivering 10 to 12 groups weekly throughout a long problematic year, come rain or shine, with or without a service manager. The premises were well located and fit for purpose. Some work had been done on programme quality and new resources had been ordered. There was a small abstinence-based group within the programme which had some well-publicized success in helping participants become abstinent from all substances.

The CAT management and the GAS monitoring officer were supportive and keen to be involved in SEA's change process. We all agreed SEA needed to begin its own journey of recovery.

---

1   Kuladharini was known at this time as Sophia Young. She was ordained as a member of the
     Western Buddhist Order in 2008 and became Dharmacarini Kuladharini.

'Firstly, put your own house in order', Kim Ross, Milestone

A handy slogan that neatly encapsulates the initial order of recovery business at SEA. Our first priority was to meet the basic requirements of contract, care standards and current thinking on what makes effective community rehabilitation. The staff wanted to feel safe and supported at work, the service users wanted a much better looking base and more organized service.

I spent the first month just watching the project in action as it was. I planned only to change the illegal and the dangerous in that time. I was looking out for what was working, how the various stakeholders interacted with the service, as well as working out possibilities for use of space. I spoke to anyone who would talk to me about their views, impressions and experiences of the project. Fortunately there was nothing illegal but, before the month was out, I had instituted an assertive communication policy to prevent a dangerous build up of misunderstandings, fear and some seething resentments. Staff member Iain McNeill had strong feelings about the way things were before the changes brought by the project's recovery; 'there was no structure, no effective challenging of the on-site situation and no safe environment or boundaries being maintained and enforced'.

The assertive communication policy contained a few basic principles guiding our interactions with each other, allowing us all to say it as we see it and at the same time be accountable to each other and open to being wrong. Crucially, this new policy applied to everyone including me.

Service User Forum Minutes 22 May 2007:

> Sophia (Kuladharini) gave notice that she had invited the staff team to be more assertive in their feedback to service users about behaviour in groups and in the common areas and that the staff are also still open to feedback about their behaviour from service users. This was welcomed after some discussion about what it would mean.

A sense of mutuality and collective accountability to each other was a first step in creating the safety so needed by the staff and service users to embark on the hazards of a rapid change process. We needed to get real, get honest with each other and be together enough as a community for this journey.

In June a new programme timetable was unveiled, clocks went up in every room and a time boundaries policy was agreed and implemented. Service User Forum Minutes 20 July 2007:

Feedback about new structure:

There was praise for new material and the new boundaries. The transition had not been easy but had been worth it. Group members have noticed that they are now getting the hang of the programme and it's all falling into place.

The time boundaries policy established a group start time and a 15-minute window for latecomers. Being a mutual policy, this meant staff members had to be on time to deliver groups and participants who arrived after the cut-off time would be refused admission. This actually increased group attendance.

The times of groups were altered to create maximum use of space and minimize the chaos of too many people in the project at one time. The timetable was simplified for each phase, making it much easier to remember. Common areas were staffed at longer break times.

This allowed for much more attention to be given to service users and reduced the fear that can come with trying to manage 20–30 sensitive people in a small space. New materials were introduced for Phases 1, 2 and 3. Each phase had clear outcomes and the programme materials focused on delivering them. Service users' progress against the outcomes was reviewed regularly in both individual sessions with key workers and in a more formal meeting with care managers.

These first structural changes created a healthier framework from which we were able to take radical steps in improving the project's physical appearance and the consistency of its systems. It is, as we say in Glasgow, 'a true fact' that strong messages about the quality of a service are given before the individual even attends or the staff open their mouths to talk about it. The environment speaks volumes, as do the kind of materials used to advertise the project as well as the quality of the resources available to do the work. SEA set about creating an atmosphere of calm, safety and beauty in which to operate. Colour, plants, art and music in every room combined to give the project that much desired 'wow' factor sought after in home improvement TV programmes. Each group room had the essential equipment installed and the accumulated debris of seven years taken out. A new 'one-to-one' room was created out of the manager's office. Team members were shifted into one office and the other was made into another small group room. So, with a more effective timetable for use of rooms and by rationalizing office space, we doubled the project's physical capacity.

'SEA has never looked so good,' said Nikki Johnston, former SEA service manager, on a visit in early 2008. In November 2007 the Care Commission visited and gave the project a clean bill of health. There were no requirements or recommendations. SEA completed its first year of recovery as a project with strong physical changes in its environment, a complete transformation in its psychological approaches and systems and with the idea of recovery as a journey; the guiding principle in all our decisions and developments

'Keep asking the questions', Kuladharini, South East Alternatives

Eric first brought that fateful Recovery resource pack to me in November 2007. I had heard about recovery before, at a TPS staff conference. To be frank, I had tuned out – not quite getting what was new in all this 'recovery' stuff – weren't we all doing it anyway? But one of the first impacts of reading that Scottish Recovery Network definition was that I began to ask the question: 'What does recovery mean to you?' I asked it in our team meeting. Team members asked it in the CAT meetings with our colleagues. We sent out a sessional worker to ask it in the reception of the local methadone clinic. We asked our own service users during their individual sessions. Service users began to build a picture in their heads of what recovery means to them – goals emerged more naturally and steps leading to the achieving of the goals suggested themselves.

At an SEA team meeting we did a huge graphic facilitation of what the project's recovery would look like to us. For me it was an image of the big room at the Adelphi Centre in the Gorbals filled to capacity with service users' friends, family and workers celebrating graduations from our programmes. (This actually happened in January 2008 – it was magnificent!)

When the notion of recovery started to embed itself in the team, it showed in our attitudes, practices and beliefs. The head-down problem-driven mindset gradually shifted to one of possibilities and potential solutions. In one of our (at the time) daily team meetings we explored how those attitudes and beliefs about addiction shape how we design a service. We asked ourselves, how exactly we were helping and how we were hindering individual recovery journeys. We recognized that even if someone attended everything and did all the homework, they still might not get better and asked where that leaves our view of ourselves as a service. Taking into account the fact that service user compliance plus our new programme content doesn't equal a cure from addiction, means dropping the view that we might have all the answers.

We began to see that we were not the star player in someone's recovery but a very small bit player trying our best to make a good enough contribution. There was freedom in handing back responsibility to the service users for their recovery journey.

What remained was our responsibility to use the public resources given to us to the best effect possible for the people we serve. We agreed that as a community rehabilitation service the public has the right to ask us to help people stop using substances. We asked, 'Is it good enough to start our rehabilitation programme on methadone and end it on the same "doze" a year later?' We wondered, 'Does harm-reduction and person-centred planning mean we can't set outcomes or goals for programmes?' and, 'How do we help people who can't meet the outcomes? Is it right just to end the programme for someone?'

Staying open to the questions means we are not dogmatically tied to any one view of how recovery should progress. We continue to embrace both 12-step and harm reduction approaches. We can also admit it when what we are doing is making the situation worse.

We continue to experiment with many answers to these questions and, layer by layer, we are building groups and systems that contribute more fully to service users' recovery process. In addition to our three-phase programmes, we create tailored short programmes for some individuals who need additional help to meet the outcomes for the programme. They also work for those who relapse after completing a programme successfully and return to the service for another round of programmed support with us. Each of those short programmes is focused on the precise area that is assessed to be the source of the difficulty. We draw from existing groups and our library of manuals and help books to construct a meaningful short intervention with an intention that, on completion, the service user will join the next phase of the main programme. So for example, a successful 1.5 would help someone enter Phase 2, a successful 2.5 would allow access to Phase 3, etc.

Combining flexibility with clarity in this way has been helpful in that we can provide more channels for any momentum a service user may have towards recovery while not compromising the safety of the group programme. We want people to think of recovery when they think of

SEA, so the first question we ask at our daily visits slots for potential service users is, 'What does recovery mean to you?'

'Build communities of recovery', Jacqui Johnston-Lynch, Sharp, Liverpool

I had been continually struck during 2008 by the fact that we are a *community* rehabilitation service. What did that mean? How do whole communities heal? How do we make a contribution to that healing?

In 2007 Netta Maciver, then chief executive of TPS, suggested that I look at creating opportunities for celebrating success in the project. Our first graduation happened in August of that year. While I was prepared for the effect graduations might have on the service users (their delight and that of their loved ones is apparent in the photos), I was totally surprised by the very positive effect it had on the SEA team and our referring care managers. It seems that we also need to remember that people do get better and to lift up our heads from the daily grind and to celebrate recovery.

The SEA graduation ceremony is growing as a community event. Three times a year we personally invite service users, their families, friends, care managers, colleagues, as well as representatives from local community organizations and local businesses to witness local recovery journeys. There is no press coverage of this event. This is a deliberate policy based on a belief that individuals take more notice of first-hand, direct experience than they do of the media. So far it's working. The event has intimacy, emotional intensity and packs a powerful message of recovery, as person after person gets up to receive their graduation certificate and share a little of what they have achieved. Those who attend as witnesses are asked to speak up in their own communities about what they have seen of recovery from addiction.

Another exploration of how communities heal came as a result of some informal research in Castlemilk. Working jointly with our CAT colleagues there, we set up immediate access to SEA at the point of their addiction clinic. We set up a Phase 1 programme in Castlemilk itself to improve the take-up rates of service. At that time there were concerns that CAT members were not referring people and CAT members were concerned that SEA was ineffective at engaging the referrals they did send to SEA. There were questions too around the location of the project – was it too far from Castlemilk really to offer a service? This ball of who-was-at-fault could have been batted back and forth for years. Instead we met it head on, and were open to the fact that we might be failing to engage people effectively. So the informal research was launched. What we found was not a culprit or a system failure but that there was an enormous failure of hope. A failure of hope, in service users themselves, that recovery was possible for them. Staff in CATs and SEA had noticed it as individual phenomena but, until we jointly undertook the work, never put it together as a generalized experience. We wondered how to respond to that. SEA hosted a tea party.

I called and invited colleagues from addiction services, family support services and fellowships in the south east of Glasgow to share a cup of tea and cake. We asked ourselves what does recovery mean to us? The meeting concluded harmoniously an hour later with a commitment to return in a month's time with service user representatives. We met over the next six months to share thoughts and ideas about how we can develop hope that recovery is possible in the south east of Glasgow and that there are services and supports to help people do that. The culmination of these tea parties was an experimental conversation café where 40 representatives of service users, service providers, fellowships and family members met in St Andrews on the Square (a restored church in the centre of Glasgow which provides space for functions and organized events) and asked, 'What does recovery mean to you?'

The working party is keen to roll these conversations out in smaller forms in the various communities in the south side of the city. From these conversations, some clues are emerging for me about how communities recover from addiction. Seeing how people relaxed, connected with each other and beamed at the end of the conversation café, I can see that just sharing our stories and listening to each other is a start.

SEA has embraced recovery, not just as a tool for use by service users, but in our idea of the service itself. The project is now in its third year of recovery and we are still keeping our own house in order, asking the questions and building communities of recovery. We are a work in progress.

References

Scottish Recovery Network (2009) *Raising Expectations and Sharing Ideas for Mental Health Recovery.* Glasgow: Scottish Recovery Network.

CHAPTER 4

Women in Recovery

Betsy Thom

Introduction

The concept of recovery is difficult to define, possibly because the subjective nature of the recovery process means that the experience – and what 'works' – is different for different groups of people, for each individual and for different problems. However, it is a concept which has attracted increasing attention in the mental health field and has emerged more recently in the discourse on addiction and addiction services. The chapter begins with a brief overview of how recovery has been framed within the mental health and addictions policy literature before looking at the relevance of this debate to women and recovery. The focus of the chapter is on gendered differences in the recovery process and the implications for responses aimed at supporting women. In particular, factors relating to social context, psychological and emotional characteristics and the responses of significant others are examined. The chapter raises questions about the availability of evidence which can identify positive intervention approaches and considers issues for future policy and practice.

What does recovery mean?

As pointed out by Shepherd, Boardman and Slade (2008) recovery has become the key organizing principle underlying mental health services in the UK as well as further afield in countries such as Australia, New Zealand and the US. Recognizing that the concept is contested, attempts are made in policy statements to provide a definition and a set of guiding principles to inform service provision for people with mental health problems. One document, for example, notes three distinct meanings of 'recovery': 'as a spontaneous and natural process; as a response to effective treatments and as a way of growing with or despite continuing disability' (Care Services Improvement Partnership 2007, p.vi).

In most recent policy statements, the personal experience of service users and their active involvement in defining and managing their recovery is seen as a core element in the recovery process. For instance, in 2005 the National Institute for Mental Health in England (NIMHE) issued a *Guiding Statement on Recovery* which proposed that recovery is: 'what people *experience themselves* as they become *empowered to manage their lives* in a manner that allows them to achieve a fulfilling, meaningful life and a contributing positive sense of belonging in their communities' (Foreword, NIMHE 2005, emphasis in original).

It is possible also to identify a number of common principles and themes emerging from statements on recovery from mental illness. These include acknowledging:

- the pursuit of health and wellness as the focus of the recovery process – which requires a shift in emphasis from pathology and morbidity towards health and strength

- hope and the belief in the possibility of positive change, where services provide support for change through mentoring and supervisory interventions – as opposed to delivering services to passive recipients of care – just doing something to somebody

- social inclusion – in work, family, housing, leisure and community activities

- empowerment, through giving people information and enabling them to make decisions to effect changes in their lives

- the importance of re-finding and redefining a sense of identity and self-confidence, which may have been eroded by ill health – often the first step on a recovery journey. This can be fostered through the use of positive language in framing the individual's experience of illness.

The model of recovery is, therefore, an active one, where professional power is reduced and ownership of the recovery process is passed, as far as possible, to the concerned individual (Care Services Improvement Partnership 2007; NIMHE 2005; Social Perspectives Network 2007; Shepherd *et al.* 2008).

But how do you measure and assess 'recovery'? This is an important issue in the mental health literature which goes beyond the remit of this chapter. Turning to the addictions literature, the most fundamental question – and the subject of continuing debate – relates to the goals of recovery and whether 'success' requires abstinence (as other chapters in this book will examine). In particular, abstinence models are frequently compared with harm reduction models which accept that people who continue to use drugs may still lead a fulfilling life if the harm associated with their drug use (criminal involvement, mental and physical health problems, social functioning) can be prevented or reduced. The tendency has often been to see the two approaches as alternatives rather than complementary.

Concerns arising from research findings on the provision of replacement therapy for drug users have brought the issue to the fore in the UK, resulting in considerable media coverage, with headlines such as 'Cold Turkey to Replace Methadone for Addicts' (Barnes 2008). Ashton (2008), reviewing the debate in a paper called 'The new abstentionists', documents the extent to which methadone maintenance has become a political issue and considers claims that there has been a shift away from a model of recovery aimed at supporting the individual to be drug free and too much towards a model based on long-term maintenance prescribing or maintenance for life. The article deconstructs the arguments for and against abstinence compared to harm reduction and in the process demonstrates the fragility of available evidence for either stance. It argues for policy which acknowledges the complexity of recovery and the fact that causal links between drug use and psychological and social risk factors are far from clear.

Similar debates are found within the alcohol field, where the concept of recovery is familiar to most people in the form used within 12-step programmes. According to Alcoholics Anonymous, Narcotics Anonymous and other 12-step programmes, recovery is a life-long process, individuals are 'in recovery' and abstinence from all drugs is a necessary requirement for well-being (health, emotional and social). But, despite its long history in the addictions field, there is still ambiguity and lack of consensus about the meaning of being 'in recovery'. This has stimulated recent attempts to provide a standard definition which would permit systematic measurement of recovery useful for research, policy and intervention. A statement issued by the Betty Ford Institute Consensus Panel – consisting of researchers, policy makers, treatment providers and people in recovery – proposes an operational definition of recovery as 'a voluntarily maintained lifestyle composed of sobriety, personal health, and citizenship' with the WHO Quality of Life (QOL) as a possible measurement tool (Betty Ford Institute Consensus Group 2007, p.221). But this, too, has its critics. In a commentary on the proposal, Arndt and Taylor (2007) point out the many problems inherent in the terminology used in the suggested definition, the continuing professional and public misunderstanding of the recovery process, and the possible impact on people 'in recovery' which might follow from the adoption of inappropriate measures. The authors highlight ways in which the achievements of people in recovery might be underestimated through the use of measures such as the QOL:

> A working mother in recovery for 5–10 years might only be able to find employment at a local fast food restaurant because of a previous felony drug conviction. Her financial situation might be dire, and she would not be able to afford anything but public transportation. According to the WHO-QOL, she might not be doing well. That she maintains her sobriety in the face of these hardships says otherwise. (Arndt and Taylor 2007, p.276)

There is, then, a continuing dialogue at policy and practice levels regarding the meaning of recovery from problem drug and alcohol use which has a direct impact on how substance users will experience and be affected by service structures and approaches and by professional expectations and attitudes towards service users. This is recognized in the *Essential Care* report from the Scottish Advisory Committee on Drug Misuse (SACDM) (SACDM 2008).

Essential Care borrows considerably from mental health literature in its examination of approaches and services for recovery from problem substance use. The report noted that a paradigm shift in thinking throughout Health and Social Care has resulted in a move away from 'a passive model to one regarding those being helped as active participants with services facilitating their recovery... This approach implies that people can develop strengths and skills in the face of the challenges they encounter when dealing with the chronic relapsing nature of their problem' (p.10).

A person-centred approach, aiming to empower service users, is further emphasized in the acknowledgement that: 'There are many paths to well-being and recovery and a person's attempt to deal with their substance problem is a unique and personal process' (p.7).

As in mental health policy statements, some key principles are specified which are intended to inform the development and delivery of services.

Principles of service provision

1. People with substance use problems, in common with society, have aspirations to have healthy and happy families and to experience fulfilling lives. Disadvantage, poverty and social exclusion are closely aligned with problem substance use. Services to improve health and well-being must reflect this.

2. Services must acknowledge the stigma associated with substance use. It is their duty to challenge it.

3. Recovery must become the focus of the care available for problem substance use rather than an ideology which advocates any particular type of treatment. Recovery encompasses harm reduction and abstinence.

4. All services and commissioning partners must put service users at the heart of their activities. Person-centred approaches must underpin all services.

5. All services provided to people with an alcohol or drug problem should be accessible to individuals regardless of their race, religion, gender, gender identity, sexual orientation, disability or age. Local governance and accountability processes must ensure this national drive is translated into local, effective service design and delivery.

6. Assessment must address the totality of people's lives. Recovery plans must therefore address a full range of social issues including housing, education and working aspirations, legal difficulties and health improvement. There should be a regular formal review of progress.

7. All people with problem substance use must have access to the same service as everyone else – this includes the right to be registered with a GP and to access primary health and social care services. Services must take cognisance of the full range of substance users' needs.

(SACDM 2008, p.13)

As mentioned above – and recognized in policy statements – acceptance of principles such as those recommended in *Essential Care*, and acting upon them to develop service structures and approaches, demands considerable changes from professionals and has far reaching consequences for the recovery process of substance users. But clearly, even taking account of such guidelines, service provision still has to address the heterogeneity of clients: gender, ethnicity, age, patterns and history of drug use, the particular contexts of users' lives, and so on. In this chapter, the focus is on gender and specifically on women; although it could be argued that we need to consider men and women together fully to understand gender influences on the recovery process.

Women, drugs and recovery

How service use, need for services and help seeking for problem substance use is influenced by gender has accrued a body of research. Much of the work is slanted towards examining women's life circumstances, their substance use and the relationship between the conditions of life and their use and experiences of services (e.g. Hedrich 2000; Thom and Green 1995; Waterson 2000). However, as in the case of mental health, gender issues and the possible differential impact on the lives of men and women, have not been examined in relation to shifts in thinking about recovery from problem substance use. Differences in the social and normative contexts of men's and women's lives are important considerations in operationalizing key aspirations such as: to 'facilitate a return to mainstream society' (SACDM 2008, p.6), or to 'recognise that problem substance users share their general life aspirations with other members of society' (p.8), or to 'have a shift of care from a passive model to one of regarding those being helped as active participants with services' (p.10) with 'increased self management of treatment; and greater participation in their own treatment' (p.12). While the new emphases on 'empowering' service users, facilitating their participation in the recovery process and moving towards 'self-management' sound like laudable ideals, how will they work out in practice? Are changes likely to have different consequences for men and women? It is not possible to provide answers in this chapter; but subsequent sections will draw on the research literature to illustrate some key issues which are important in providing positive experiences of the recovery process for women.

Although limited in number and scope, recent research studies have examined the needs of drug- (and alcohol-) using women entering services and examples from this literature serve to highlight the importance of taking into account gender-specific aspects of the mental and physical health of users, their social circumstances and situational contexts and the impact of responses of significant others on recovery. The studies mentioned below do not comprise a comprehensive overview; they are intended as illustrative of issues covered in the relevant literature and, as this chapter was originally presented as a seminar paper in Scotland, the findings from studies conducted in Scotland have some prominence.

The first examples present findings on the complex range of mental health problems commonly encountered in samples of drug users, reflecting the need for gender sensitivity in understanding the relationship between drug use and mental health. Next, examples from the research literature on four groups of women – sex workers, homeless women, women prisoners and women as mothers – serve to illustrate the importance of life situations and social contexts and the issues arising for specific groups.

Mental health and drug use

A study by Gilchrist, Gruer and Atkinson (2007) looked at some of the characteristics of women coming into three services in Glasgow; these were a social and medical drop in service for female street prostitutes, a drug crisis centre and a medically-led specialist service for opiate dependent users. The study found, unsurprisingly, that 71% of the women accessing the services had been emotionally abused, 65% physically abused, 50% sexually abused, 36% had deliberately self-harmed, 48% attempted suicide, and 35% had eating disorders in the past. At the time of the study, 85% of the women met the threshold for diagnosis as having a neurotic disorder and 71% reported symptoms which suggested that they needed treatment for mental health problems apart from their drug use. Figures for sexual and physical abuse were slightly higher than those from a similar study conducted in Scotland by McKeganey, Neale and Robertson (2005) which reported that among clients of drug treatment services, 35.5% of women (compared to 6.9% of men) reported sexual abuse and 61.9% of women (compared to 22.3% of men) reported physical abuse. It may be, as Gilchrist *et al.* (2007) indicate, that this was due to a relatively large proportion of their sample of women working in the sex industry. However, the identification of a 'high level of repeat victimization' and the possibility of a 'cycle of domestic violence' among women drug users in the study by McKeganey *et al.* (2005, p.230) underscores the extent to which women may enter the recovery process with a different profile of emotional and mental health needs from male drug users.

Sex work

As noted above, drug use is frequently a feature of sex work. In a study of sex workers in four Scottish cities (McKeganey 2006), 70–90% of sex workers were found to be injecting drug users. Further examination of the women's situation highlighted the reasons underpinning their initial and continuing involvement in sex work – namely that they were living in dire physical, financial and emotional circumstances. They were mainly working in order to support themselves and their children. Life was pretty bleak for these women and, for most of them, drugs provided a crutch to cope with their problems and their work. At the same time, that study also brought another interesting insight to the forefront, one that is rarely discussed or investigated. Most often, women involved in drugs and sex work and other related problems are portrayed as victims, caught in an unwanted lifestyle because they have few choices and because life is difficult. But some of the women in McKeganey's study (admittedly very few) reported that they had undertaken sex work because *they saw it* as a choice in lives characterized by loneliness and a sense that something was missing. They did not see themselves as victims – an important issue when considering the recovery process. Indeed, other research has cautioned against characterizing women sex workers and drug users as necessarily victims, showing that women make choices about how best to earn money and that drug-using lifestyles offer some women a degree of independence and sense of purpose from which they feel otherwise excluded (e.g. Taylor 1993). Research by Cusick and Hickman (2005) further enforces the importance of taking account of the social context of drug use – in this case, different sex work settings. Based on their survey of a sample of sex workers in England, they found strong associations between drug use and being 'trapped' in sex work; being engaged in outdoor/drift sex work (as opposed to working indoors) reinforced vulnerabilities and was more likely to lead to mutual reinforcement between problem drug use and sex work.

Homelessness

An association between homelessness, drug use and other mental health and social problems is well established (Neale 2001). Although women are generally less likely than men to end up 'roofless' – sleeping in the street or without shelter – the term 'homeless' incorporates those living in emergency accommodation such as hostels or bed and breakfast and those housed temporarily by relatives or acquaintances. In a study which included 63 homeless people in Scotland, Neale (2001) found four women (16 men) in emergency accommodation, one woman (17 men) 'roofless' and nine women (16 men) temporarily housed. The sample was characterized by multiple and interrelated problems (unemployment, imprisonment, mental health problems, being in care during childhood) and high levels of life-threatening behaviour. Being on the streets meant that access to health and social care services was often difficult. Similar problems emerged in a study of homeless men and women by McNaughton (2008), highlighting the effects of marginalization on opportunities to access help and manage drug use. Even once support services and a home were secured, other problems remained. As one of the women respondents remarked, 'once you have gone through the whole system and you have got your wee house and then you have done all that and everything is fine, there is nothing'. In a sense, the woman becomes trapped in a sort of limbo, where there is nothing to replace the loss of the contacts and routines which fill the life of an active drug user. As homeless women may be less visible than homeless men – because they are less often found on the streets – the specific gender-related factors influencing the recovery process are unclear and this is an area which requires investigation.

Imprisonment

Typically, women prisoners have been found to have high levels of drug and alcohol dependence, social and mental health problems, to have experienced high levels of past abuse and violence, and to suffer from low self-esteem (e.g. Borrill et al. 2003; HM Prison Service 2008, 2009; Malloch 2000). Recent figures show that up to 80% of women in English prisons have diagnosable mental health problems, with 66% having symptoms of neurotic disorders (anxiety, poor sleeping); the comparable figure in the community is less than 20%. Up to 50% of women in prison report having experienced physical, emotional or sexual abuse.

In 2006, 33% of sentenced women had committed drugs offences. The incidence of self-injury is significantly high; since 2003, approximately 30% of female prisoners self-injured each year (compared to 6% of males) (HM Prison Service 2009). Two-thirds of women prisoners are mothers and are more likely than men to be single parents or the main carers of children. Only 5% of children stay in their own homes after the imprisonment of their mother (HM Prison Service 2008).

Drawing on research, one report on women prisoners in England documented evidence of unmet need for treatment services and for ongoing support within prisons and beyond. In particular, women prisoners indicated that they wanted longer and more consistent detoxification services and other forms of support. They were dissatisfied that the response to their depression, anxiety and other emotional needs was often medication, while they would have preferred just having someone to talk to (Borrill *et al.* 2003). The same study also highlighted different sub-cultural patterns of drug use among the women, indicating the importance of cultural as well as gender sensitivity in recovery pathways. Problems specific to women prisoners' recovery process have been recognized as part of a new Gender Equality Duty in guidance notes on Gender-Specific Standards for care in prisons (HM Prison Service 2008). Such guidance notes suggest awareness of women's social contexts outside as well as inside prison and of how recovery is influenced by social expectations, ascribed roles (as wives and mothers) and definitions of 'femininity'. But Malloch (2000, p.147) adds a further dimension when she argues that, 'female drug users in prison are at an intersection of a range of intrusive discourses, which are aimed at controlling behaviour and ensuring conformity' which means that 'women become the focus for a wide range of normalising techniques'. That is, the recovery process for women is seen as getting women back into being good mothers, good wives, good carers, good workers – fulfilling the expected roles and responsibilities which may have been a source of, or closely linked to, drug use in the first place. Of course, it is not just drug users in prison who are at an intersection of intrusive 'normalizing' interventions but also female drug users within other settings, including treatment services. Women who become pregnant and drug-using mothers are another good example of a group which is subject to multiple pressures including identity transition from one social status to another while they attempt to recover from drug use.

Motherhood

There is a significant amount of work which examines drug use, pregnancy and motherhood, although with few exceptions (e.g. Klee, Jackson and Lewis 2002; Woods 2007) the focus is on clinical issues, management and the effects of use on the foetus. Woods (2007), however, based her account of drug use and motherhood on the experiences of drug-using women, professional workers and family members in Dublin and described drug use and motherhood within conditions of social exclusion and family adversity. In analysing the process of becoming a mother, Woods looked at the trajectory of motherhood from early learning experiences in the family of origin to becoming a mother for the first time, examining how different experiences of the mothering role intersect with drug-using 'careers' and social contexts. In the Dublin study (as in other research) many women drug users had problematic backgrounds of one sort or another, and sometimes that involved being the carer in the family. The women, themselves, had been 'little mothers' looking after their siblings and sometimes their parents. Thus they adopted a particular kind of mother 'identity' at an early age. Later decisions, to become pregnant and to become mothers themselves, involved an identity change at each of those transitions, a role change which was often met with hostility and disapproval from other people because of their drug use. While all women who become mothers have to come to terms with their new identity, for drug users it is much more difficult because of stereotypical images held by many significant others and professional carers alike – 'aha, drug users, bad mother' or 'we must watch out for the children' or 'she shouldn't really be getting pregnant'. Being able to adopt and adjust to the identity of mother becomes more difficult and these parallel and shifting identities of 'mother' and 'drug user' need to be taken into account as women enter and progress through the recovery cycle.

Challenges: Overcoming stereotypes and taking control of the recovery process

From the above examples it is clear that recovery pathways and processes for women are influenced by many of the same factors which influence the recovery of male drug users: the availability of accessible, appropriate support systems, services and social networks. But what counts as available, appropriate and supportive is likely to be gender specific to a greater or lesser extent depending on the circumstances and life experiences of the individual.

Many stereotypes exist about drug-using women. They are viewed as 'bad', because they use drugs and/or alcohol in the first place. They are 'sad' because they are victims of circumstances and of dependence on the men in their lives. Or they are 'mad', worse than male drug users, because nothing can be done to help them and their prognosis is bad. These stereotypes are reflected in the literature (e.g. discussed in Hedrich 2000; Perry 1979) although increasingly challenged (see Ettorre 2004; United Nations Office on Drugs and Crime (UNODC) 2004). However, as Ettorre (2004, p.328) has argued, we still 'need "to revision" our notions and concepts' of women drug users. As mentioned earlier, men's recovery process is also subject to gender-related pressures; but, 'women are at a greater disadvantage because "masculinist" (i.e. male privileging)...and paternalistic epistemologies predominate' (Ettorre 2004, p.330). These 'paternalistic epistemologies' or 'ways of seeing' are reflected in the goals and aspirations held out to women by helping agents as essential elements of the recovery process. It could be argued that very often, aspirations located in social roles of mother, wife, partner and carer are images that professionals, drug workers and society in general deem appropriate, rather than those to which women users themselves aspire. In prison and treatment settings and in other services which women may access for help, the structures and social arrangements frequently operate to institutionalize male domination and the male hierarchy as it operates in a particular society or cultural group. Tension between care and control is perhaps more obvious and visible in those settings where 'rehabilitation' is predicated on the acceptance of a vision of recovery which emphasizes values and lifestyles from which women have tried to escape in the first place. As is recognized in the SACDM (2008) report – although not with specific reference to women – to provide an appropriate foundation for the recovery process requires challenging public and professional views of women and drug use, tackling the social situational factors which affect recovery and changing institutional structures which limit opportunities for women to progress through the recovery process. These same factors operate to constrain the extent to which the ideals of empowering women to take greater control of the recovery process can be achieved:

> services can make service users into passive recipients of interventions which are organised, not around their hopes, wishes

and aspirations, but around the needs of services to develop systems which meet high levels of demand and manage risk. This approach is rarely person-centred. (SACDM 2008, p.9)

To some extent, these issues have been examined in research on access to services and service provision for women substance users and similar themes have emerged from work in different countries. International reviews (Hedrich 2000; UNODC 2004; European Monitoring Centre for Drugs and Drug Addiction (EMCDDA) 2005) have supported findings mentioned above that the profile of women coming into treatment differs from that of men in terms of their demographics, their patterns of substance use, and the nature and severity of the problems they present. Despite differences of culture, socio-economic and policy structures and service provision, gender-related difficulties, such as stigma and shame, lack of family or supportive networks, living with a using partner, experience of abuse in childhood and later life, are commonly reported from many countries. Challenging stereotypes, and the ways in which they are reflected in service provision and professional and public attitudes towards women's recovery, remains a major task if ownership of the recovery process is to be shared more equally with women drug users. Access to treatment and engagement in treatment are only part of the recovery process; nevertheless, since this is the aspect of recovery which has received most research attention so far, it is worth drawing out some of the main research findings.

Service provision for women

The review from UNODC (2004), *Substance Abuse Treatment and Care for Women: Case Studies and Lessons Learned,* divided the barriers to accessing and engaging in treatment into three main categories: 1. social, cultural and personal; 2. structural; 3. systemic.

Social, cultural and personal barriers

Social, cultural and personal barriers arise from women's social roles, social expectations of appropriate female behaviour, attitudes towards women with problems of drug use and frequently, women's lack of empowerment and their disadvantaged life circumstances. Much of this has been discussed in previous sections. For many women, substance use may have started as, or become, a way of self-medication and coping with expectations they were unable to meet. Feelings of stigma and shame, fear of sanctions from family members as well as the public and fear of losing custody of children commonly operate to prevent women seeking help for drug use. Many drug-using women are separated from their partners; others are living with a drug-using partner who is not always supportive of the woman seeking treatment. Thus admitting to the drug problem and seeking help – an essential first step in the recovery process – is hampered.

Structural barriers

Structural barriers at the policy and practice level impede efforts to access help not just from specialist drug services but from other sources of help and support – such as general health care, employment or housing. These include waiting lists and the capacity of services to respond to demand which may mean that the recovery process is hindered even when women have sought help. Research has provided many examples of structural barriers and the following selected issues of 'safe environments' and 'childcare provision' are indicative. The extent to which services are seen as safe for women is an important consideration with implications not just for the external location of the service but for the design of the interior space and the operation of the programme elements, for instance, the provision of women-only sessions. Service environments have been criticized as male dominated, perpetuating traditional male and female roles and traditional views of feminine behaviour which may result in women experiencing sexual harassment or even violence within treatment settings.

Reviews have reported women-centred treatment approaches which included women-only components as conducive to positive outcomes, including fostering self-confidence, empowerment and a positive sense of identity (see review in Hedrich 2000).

Policies to reduce harm and ensure safety outside service provision are also important but not without contention. For example, one of the issues in McKeganey's (2006) work on sex workers in Scotland, was the question of tolerance zones in cities. Women often viewed these tolerance zones as being safer areas to work with the added benefit that services can access women relatively easily. On the other hand, it could be argued that having a tolerance zone just perpetuates the 'trap' of sex work (Cusick and Hickman 2005). So there are dilemmas in thinking through what kind of approach is taken for women in different life situations and how that affects their recovery and their aspirations for recovery.

For pregnant women, past experience of unsympathetic service staff and judgemental attitudes towards their pregnancy act as disincentives to accessing services and staying engaged in treatment. But the most frequently reported barrier is inadequate childcare provision or none at all. There are dilemmas for both women users and service providers in deciding how to address the fact that women, more often than men, are lone parents and that the demands of treatment programmes – for regular attendance, keeping to rigid appointment times, attending at a particular venue – may require consideration of the needs of children of different ages. Residential services which enable women to take their children into the residence with them, and day care or crèche provision attached to treatment services, seem like an appropriate, useful approach, although provision of a crèche may not suit some service users with older children and more flexibility in attendance demands or in types of assistance is preferable. At the same time, women are not always happy to bring small children to services even where facilities are provided. Drawing on a small sample of interviews which I carried out with women drug and alcohol users during the late 1980s (unpublished work), some of the women in residential treatment appreciated the opportunity to be without their children in order to concentrate on their own recovery. Although concerned about separation from their children, they were also unsure that a drug rehabilitation environment was good for them. Equally, women attending day care centres or other specialist services expressed doubts about whether it was a suitable place for children. Clearly the issue of childcare is not straightforward; it poses dilemmas for women drug users and service providers which are likely to require a range of different solutions depending on the age of children and the women's recovery stage, as well as a range of other factors.

Systemic barriers

Systemic barriers arise from the wider social structures which determine the levels of participation in public life, the extent to which women are included or excluded from decision making positions at all levels of society, the institutionalization of beliefs and ideas which are gender insensitive and the extent to which women, themselves, have internalized beliefs and attitudes which sustain their positions of powerlessness and dependency. One example given in the UNODC report (2004, p.18) is the need for interventions aiming to change high-risk behaviour such as needle sharing or non-use of condoms to take account of unequal power relationships between men and women which make negotiation about high-risk behaviours difficult for women. An important point made in the report (p.18) is that, because most women have multiple needs which can rarely be met within one agency, 'models for collaboration, partnering and service agreements need to be researched and developed'. A 'partnership' approach to service provision has become a feature of UK policy generally and is reflected in policies to address problems associated with substance use, including in *Essential Care* (SACDM 2008). Such an approach has the possibility to tackle systemic disadvantages for women drug users but, at the same time, may run the risk of increasing the potential for women to be caught in the net of intersecting, intrusive interventions and normalization demands more likely to increase than diminish feelings of low self-esteem and powerlessness. Again, this is an area for further investigation.

Conclusion

'Recovery' has become a key concept in rethinking policy and practice approaches to treatment and support for drug users. Although there remains considerable debate about the meaning of 'recovery', a core element of the new thinking is the belief that drug users should be treated as active participants in decisions regarding their recovery and empowered to manage the recovery process as far as possible. Guidelines for the provision of treatment and support services embody sets of principles designed to move towards the 'active' recovering individual, and reduce professional ownership of the process and professional control of recovery aspirations. There is, however, still some way to go in examining not only the concept of 'recovery' and how it can be put into practice, but also the meaning and significance for different groups of drug users of the guiding principles and of setting up 'empowerment' or 'person-centred services' or self-management as ideals. For instance, taking on even partial responsibility for, and ownership of, the recovery process may present women with additional challenges which they are unable to meet at some stages of the recovery cycle.

In discussing the creation of a UK Recovery Academy, Best and Bamber (2009) make an important point when they state that, 'There was a concern that recovery is not the aim for many people, and that "discovery" was a much more appropriate term than "recovery" to describe the transcendence to something much better than life before addiction.' This may be especially true for women, one (heterogeneous) group where research specific to recovery as it is now framed is lacking. Existing research, in the UK and internationally, has shown that gender factors are important; women present to specialist treatment services or enter prison or appear at other agencies with a different profile of drug use and associated problems from men and, as sections above have shown, they face particular hurdles to recovery arising from their own life contexts, from the attitudes of professionals and the public to women drug users, and from the internalized and systemic disadvantages which work against the principles now embodied in treatment policies. It is imperative, therefore, to extend the debate on what 'recovery' actually means to different groups of people, to consider the possibility that there may be unwanted consequences for some groups or some individuals and to investigate and include the views of drug users themselves.

References

Arndt, S. and Taylor, P. (2007) 'Commentary on "Defining and Measuring 'Recovery'"'. *Journal of Substance Abuse Treatment 33*, 275–276.

Ashton, M. (2008) 'The new abstentionists.' *Druglink* (Special Insert), Dec/Jan 2008.

Barnes, E. (2008) 'Cold Turkey to Replace Methadone for Addicts.' *Scotland on Sunday*, 10 February. Available at http://scotlandonsunday.scotsman.com/drugspolicy/Cold-turkey-to-replace-methadone.3762513.jp (accessed September 2009).

Best, D. and Bamber, S. (2009) 'A new way.' *Drinkanddrugsnews*, 13 July. Available at www.drink-anddrugsnews.com (accessed 14 December 2009).

Betty Ford Institute Consensus Group (2007) 'What is recovery? A working definition from the Betty Ford Institute.' *Journal of Substance Abuse Treatment 33*, 221–228.

Borrill, J., Maden, A., Martin, A., Weaver, T., Stimson, G., Barnes, T., Burnett, R., Miller, S., Briggs, T. and Farrell, M. (2003) *The Substance Misuse Treatment Needs of Minority Prisoner Groups: Women, Young Offenders and Ethnic Minorities.* Home Office Development and Practice Report 8. London: Home Office.

Care Services Improvement Partnership (2007) *A Common Purpose: Recovery in Future Mental Health Services.* Social Care Institute for Excellence, Royal College of Psychiatrists and Care Services Improvement Partnership, Joint Position paper 08. Leeds: CSIP. Available at www.scie.org.uk/publications/positionpapers/pp08.pdf (accessed September 2009).

Cusick, L. and Hickman, M. (2005) '"Trapping" in drug use and sex work careers.' *Drugs: Education, Prevention and Policy 12*, 369–379.

Ettorre, E. (2004) 'Revisioning women and drug use: Gender sensitivity, embodiment and reducing harm.' *International Journal of Drug Policy 15*, 327–335.

European Monitoring Centre for Drugs and Drug Addiction (EMCDDA) (2005) *Differences in Patterns of Drug Use between Women and Men*. Lisbon: European Monitoring Centre for Drugs and Drug Abuse.

Gilchrist, G., Gruer, L. and Atkinson, J. (2007) 'Predictors of neurotic symptom severity among female drug users in Glasgow, Scotland.' *Drugs: Education, Prevention and Policy 14*, 347–365.

Hedrich, D. (2000) *Problem Drug Use by Women. Focus on Community-Based Interventions*. Strasbourg: Pompidou Group.

HM Prison Service (2008) *Women Prisoners*. Prison Service Order 4800. Available at http://pso.hmprisonservice.gov.uk/PSO_4800_women_prisoners.doc (accessed September 2009).

HM Prison Service (2009) *Female Prisoners*. Available at www.hmprisonservice.gov.uk/adviceand-support/prison_life/femaleprisoners (accessed September 2009).

Klee, H., Jackson, M. and Lewis, S. (eds) (2002) *Drug Misuse and Motherhood*. London: Routledge.

Malloch, M.S. (2000) *Women, Drugs and Custody: The Experiences of Women Drug Users in Prison*. Winchester: Waterside Press.

McKeganey, N. (2006) 'Street prostitution in Scotland: The views of working women.' *Drugs: Education, Prevention and Policy 13*, 151–166.

McKeganey, N., Neale, J. and Robertson, M. (2005) 'Physical and sexual abuse among drug users contacting drug treatment services in Scotland.' *Drugs: Education, Prevention and Policy 12*, 223–232.

McNaughton, C.C. (2008) 'Transitions through homelessness, substance use, and the effect of material marginalization and psychological trauma.' *Drugs: Education, Prevention and Policy 15*, 177–188.

National Institute for Mental Health in England (2005) *NIMHE Guiding Statement on Recovery*. London: Department of Health. Available at www.psychminded.co.uk/news/news2005/feb05/nimherecovstatement.pdf (accessed September 2009).

Neale, J. (2001) 'Homelessness amongst drug users: A double jeopardy explored.' *International Journal of Drug Policy 12*, 353–369.

Perry, L. (1979) *Women and Drug Use. An Unfeminine Dependency*. London: Institute for the Study of Drug Dependence.

Scottish Advisory Committee on Drugs Misuse (SACDM) (2008) *Essential Care: A Report on the Approach Required to Maximise Opportunity for Recovery from Problem Substance Use in Scotland*. Edinburgh: Scottish Advisory Committee on Drug Misuse. Crown copyright.

Shepherd, G., Boardman, J. and Slade, M. (2008) *Making Recovery a Reality*. Policy Paper. London: Sainsbury Centre for Mental Health.

Social Perspectives Network (2007) *Whose Recovery Is It Anyway?* Social Perspectives Network, in partnership with the Delivering Race Equality Programme, Social Care Institute for Excellence and the Sexual Orientation and Gender Identity Advisory Group. Paper 11. Available at www.spn.org.uk/fileadmin/SPN_uploads/Documents/Papers/SPN_Papers/Recovery_and_Diversity_Booklet.pdf (accessed September 2009).

Taylor, A. (1993) *Women Drug Users: An Ethnography of a Female Injecting Community*. Oxford: Oxford University Press.

Thom, B. and Green, A. (1995) 'Services for Women: The Way Forward.' In L. Harrison (ed.) *Alcohol Problems and Community Care*. London: Routledge.

United Nations Office on Drugs and Crime (UNODC) (2004) *Substance Abuse Treatment and Care for Women: Case Studies and Lessons Learned*. Vienna: UNODC.

Waterson, J. (2000) *Women and Alcohol in Social Context. Mother's Ruin Revisited*. Basingstoke: Palgrave.

Woods, M. (2007) '"Keeping Mum": A qualitative study of women drug users' experience of preserving motherhood in Dublin.' Thesis, Trinity College, Dublin.

CHAPTER 5

The Therapeutic Community: A Recovery-Oriented Treatment Pathway and the Emergence of a Recovery-Oriented Integrated System

George De Leon

Arguably, the therapeutic community (TC) for addictions is one of the first formal treatment approaches that is explicitly recovery oriented. Surely, Alcoholics Anonymous (AA) and similar mutual self-help approaches facilitate recovery but these represent themselves as support, not treatment. Pharmacological approaches, notably methadone maintenance, have as their treatment goal the reduction or elimination of illicit opiate use and evidence-based behavioural approaches, such as cognitive behavioural therapy (CBT), contingency contracting and motivational enhancement therapy (MET), focus upon reduction in targeted drug use.

In the TC perspective, however, the *primary* goal of treatment is recovery, which is broadly defined as changes in lifestyle and identity. These changes involve abstinence from all non-prescribed drug use, elimination of social deviance and development of prosocial behaviours and values (De Leon 2000). Thus the TC's unique social psychological treatment approach – community as method – is designed to address change in the 'whole person'.

Over some four decades, research and clinical experience has demonstrated that recovery occurs in considerable numbers of individuals treated in TCs and has illuminated insights as to the recovery process itself. This chapter presents the essential elements of the TC approach and its implications for developing system-wide recovery-oriented pathways.

The therapeutic community perspective and method

The TC can be distinguished from other major drug treatment modalities in two fundamental ways. First, the TC offers a systematic treatment approach that is guided by an explicit perspective on the *drug use disorder, the person, recovery and right living.* Second, the primary 'therapist' and teacher in the TC is the *community* itself, which consists of the social environment, peers and staff who, as role models of successful personal change, serve as guides in the recovery process. Thus the community is both the context in which change occurs, and the method for facilitating change. (For a detailed exposition of TC elements see De Leon 2000.)

View of the disorder

Drug abuse is regarded as a disorder of the whole person. Although individuals differ in choice of substance, abuse involves some or all the areas of functioning. Cognitive, behavioural and mood disturbances appear, as do medical problems. Thinking may be unrealistic or disorganized. Values are confused, non-existent or antisocial. Frequently there are deficits in verbal, reading, writing and marketable skills, and, whether couched in existential or psychological terms, moral issues are apparent.

Physical addiction or dependency must be seen in the wider context of the individual's psychological status and lifestyle. For some abusers, physiological factors may be important but for most these remain minor relative to the social and psychological problems which precede and the behavioural deficits that accumulate with continued substance abuse. Thus, the problem is the person, not the drug. Addiction is a symptom, not the essence of the disorder. In the TC, chemical detoxification is a condition of entry, not a goal of treatment. Sobriety is a prerequisite for changing lifestyles and identity.

View of the person

Rather than drug-use patterns, individuals are distinguished along dimensions of psychological dysfunction and social deficits. Regardless of individual differences, substance abusers share important similarities. All reveal some problems in socialization, cognitive/emotional skills and in overall psychological development evident in their immaturity, poor self-esteem, conduct and character disorder, or antisocial characteristics.

Typical features include low tolerance for all forms of discomfort and delay of gratification, inability to manage feelings (particularly hostility, guilt and anxiety); poor impulse control (particularly sexual or aggressive), poor judgement and reality testing concerning consequences of actions; unrealistic self-appraisal in terms of a discrepancy between personal resources and aspirations; prominence of lying, manipulation and deception as coping behaviours; problems with authority, personal and social irresponsibility, i.e. inconsistency or failures in completing expected obligations, and persistent difficulties in managing guilt. Additionally, significant numbers have marked deficits in education and in marketable communication skills.

Whether antecedent or consequent to serious drug involvement, these clinical characteristics are commonly observed to be correlated with chemical dependency. More importantly, TCs require a positive change in these as essential for stable recovery. Thus, all clients in TC-oriented treatment follow the same regime. Individual differences are recognized in specific treatment plans that modify the steps, not the course, of the client's experience in the TC.

View of right living

TCs adhere to certain precepts and values as essential to self-help recovery, social learning, personal growth and healthy living. Some precepts specifically orient the individual to the priority and meaning of self-help recovery. For example, they stress the personal present (here and now) as opposed to the historical past (there and then). Past behaviour and circumstances are explored only to illustrate the current patterns of dysfunctional behaviour, negative attitudes and outlook. Individuals are encouraged and trained to assume personal responsibility for their present reality and their future destiny.

The view of right living also emphasizes explicit values which guide how individuals relate to themselves, peers, significant others and the larger society. These include, for example, truth and honesty (in word and deed), the work ethic, learning to learn, personal accountability, economic self-reliance, responsible concern to others, peers ('brother's/ sister's keeper'), family responsibility, community involvement and good citizenry.

The ideological and psychological views of TC perspective are integrated into its teachings and method to achieve its main social and psychological goals. For example, the requirement of truth and honesty in all matters in the TC counters the manipulation and deception character features of many substance abusers; the stated values of accountability and social responsibility are integral teachings in training habilitation and socialization. Acquiring vocational or educational skills and social productivity is motivated by the values of achievement and self-reliance; healthy behavioural alternatives to drug use are reinforced by commitment to the values of abstinence. More generally, sobriety is a prerequisite for learning to live right but right living is required to maintain sobriety.

View of recovery

In the TC the aims of treatment are global. The primary psychological goal is to change the negative patterns of behaviour, thinking and feeling that predispose drug use; the main social goal is to develop a responsible, drug-free lifestyle. Achievement of these social and psychological goals defines recovery. Conduct, emotions, skills, attitudes and values must be integrated to ensure enduring change in lifestyle and a positive personal social identity. These goals shape the TC treatment regime as well as defining several broad assumptions concerning its view of recovery.

RECOVERY IS A DEVELOPMENTAL PROCESS

Change in the TC can be understood as a passage through stages of incremental learning. The learning that occurs at each stage facilitates change at the next, and each change reflects movement toward the goals of recovery.

MOTIVATION

Recovery depends on pressures to change, positive and negative. Some clients seek help, driven by stressful external pressures. Others are moved by more intrinsic factors. For all, however, remaining in treatment requires continued motivation to change. Thus elements of the approach are designed to sustain motivation or detect early signs of premature termination. Although the influence of treatment depends on the person's motivation and readiness, change does not occur in a vacuum. Recovery unfolds as an interaction between the client and the therapeutic environment.

SELF-HELP AND MUTUAL SELF-HELP

Strictly speaking, treatment is not provided but made available to the individual in the TC environment, in its staff and peers, the daily regime of work, groups, meetings, seminars and recreation. However, the effectiveness of these elements is dependent upon the individual, who must fully engage in the treatment regime. Self-help recovery means that the individual makes the main contribution to the change process. And mutual self-help emphasizes the fact that each individual in the process contributes to the change in others. The main messages of recovery, personal growth and right living are mediated by peers through confrontation and sharing in groups, by example as role models, and as supportive encouraging friends in daily interactions.

SOCIAL LEARNING

Negative behavioural patterns, attitudes and dysfunctional roles were not acquired in isolation, nor can they be changed in isolation. Therefore recovery depends not only on what has been learned, but on how, where and with whom learning occurs. This assumption is the basis for the community itself serving as healer and teacher. Learning occurs by doing and participating as a community member; a socially responsible role is acquired by acting the role. Changes in lifestyle and identity are gradually learned through participating in the varied roles of community life, supported by the people and relationships involved in the learning process. And, without these relationships, newly learned ways of coping are threatened by isolation and its potential for relapse. Thus, a positive perspective on self, society and a life philosophy must be affirmed by a network of others to assure a stable recovery.

Community as method

The quintessential treatment element of the TC is community. What distinguishes the TC from other treatment approaches (and other communities) is the *purposive use of the community to facilitate social and psychological change in individuals with substance abuse and related problems.* Community as method means integrating people and practices under a common perspective and purpose – to teach individuals to use the community to change themselves. Thus, all activities are designed to produce therapeutic and educational change in the individual participants and all participants are mediators of these therapeutic and educational changes.

The term 'therapeutic community' connotes that community is the method to pursue the therapeutic goals that define recovery. Community as a method can be understood in terms of *four* interrelated components. It provides the physical, social and psychological *context* for individuals to change themselves, i.e. the peer and staff relationships, the daily regimen of activities and the teachings of right living. It sets the *expectations*, the standards, for how individuals participate in this context. It continually *assesses* and *responds*, affirmatively and/or correctively, to the individual's progress in meeting these expectations. A fundamental assumption of community as method is that the process of recovery (change in lifestyle and identity) unfolds when individuals continually strive to meet community expectations. The recovery process continues beyond treatment as individuals use what they have learned in the TC to constructively engage the challenges of 'living right' in the world.

The effectiveness of the therapeutic community

Four decades of research have provided a considerable scientific knowledge base on the addiction TC. (See overviews in De Leon 1999, 2008.) This section briefly summarizes the evidence supporting the conclusions concerning the effectiveness of TC as a recovery-oriented treatment. In accordance with this objective the evidence is summarized from several areas of research: field effectiveness outcome studies, meta-analytic surveys and cost-benefit analyses, and indirect evidence from research outside TCs.

Field effectiveness

Follow-up studies have assessed social and psychological outcomes of thousands of former admissions one to 12 years after their treatment in TCs. These studies document that long-term residential TCs are effective in reducing drug abuse and antisocial behaviour, particularly in opioid abusers. The extent of improvement is directly related to retention in treatment. The longer clients remain in treatment, the greater the improvement at follow-up (De Leon 1984, 1999). In the studies that investigated psychological outcomes, such as depression, anxiety and self-concept, results uniformly showed significant improvement at follow-up (De Leon 1999).

Statistical meta-analyses

Four published studies utilized meta-analytic techniques to assess the effectiveness of TC treatment relative to a comparison condition (Lees, Manning and Rawlings 2004; Lipton *et al.* 2004; Mitchell, Wilson and MacKenzie 2006; Smith, Gates and Foxcroft 2006). These examined collections of studies that involved individual TC programmes which met certain selection criteria, mainly inclusion of a comparison or control condition. With one exception (Smith *et al.* 2006) in all of the surveys the authors conclude that the addiction TCs yield significantly better outcomes than the comparison condition.

Economic studies

Assessments of community-based TCs all report positive cost-benefit findings particularly in reducing costs associated with crime and increased benefits associated with employment (e.g. Ernst and Young 1996; Harwood *et al.* 1988, 1994; Harwood, Foundation and Livermore 1998). Additionally, fiscal studies of TCs for special populations of substance abusers with co-occurring disorders in community-based and prison settings support the conclusion that the modified TC programme could be an effective mechanism to *reduce* the costs of service utilization as well as *improve* clinical outcomes (e.g. Griffith *et al.* 1999; McGeary *et al.* 2000; French *et al.* 2000; Pearson and Lipton 1999).

Social-psychological evidence

Although TCs emerged without a formal theory, familiar social-psychological and behavioural learning principles are embedded in community as method. For example, social role training, vicarious learning, behaviour modification (i.e. reinforcement and the privileges/sanction system) are principles which are *naturalistically mediated* in therapeutic communities. An extensive research literature documents the validity of these principles, providing indirect evidence for the TC as a unique, social-psychological treatment approach.

In summary, the weight of the evidence from all sources supports the conclusion that the TC is an effective and cost-effective treatment for certain subgroups of substance abusers, particularly those with severe drug use, social and psychological problems.

The diversity of treatment communities

The effectiveness of treatments such as TCs does not necessarily solve the problem of widespread use and abuse of drugs. Substance abuse and related problems remain pervasive, with a great diversity of users and drugs of abuse. In response TCs have modified their practices and adapted the approach for special populations, settings and funding requirements. Current applications include TC programmes for adolescents, homeless substance abusers, those with co-occurring psychiatric disorders, criminal justice substance abusers, women and children, and clients maintained on methadone. Client differences, as well as clinical requirements and funding realities, have encouraged the development of modified residential TCs with shorter planned durations of stay (3, 6 and 12 months), as well as TC-oriented day treatment and outpatient ambulatory models.

Current modifications are practices, services and strategies that have been incorporated into the TC approach, which, however, retains its unique element, 'community as method'. Family services include family therapy, counselling and psycho-education. Primary health care and medical services are offered for the growing number of residential patients with sexually transmitted diseases and conditions that compromise the immune system, including HIV sero-positivity, AIDS, syphilis and hepatitis C. Mental health services include psychopharmacologic adjuncts and individual psychotherapy. Other evidence-based practices are used, such as cognitive restructuring, relapse prevention training and motivational interviewing. Twelve-step components may be introduced at any stage in residential treatment but are considered mandatory in the re-entry and aftercare stages beyond residential treatment (see De Leon 1997 for illustrative examples of adaptations and modifications).

Effectiveness of the diversity of therapeutic communities

The main populations studied have been those with co-occurring psychiatric disorders, adolescents, homeless, criminal justice clients, mothers with children, as well as clients maintained on methadone. The weight of the evidence from studies indicates that current standard and modified TCs provide effective treatment for the current generation of substance abusers, who reveal a wide range of social and psychological problems (De Leon 1999, 2008). Based upon its unique mutual self-help perspective, the TC offers a favourable, cost-effective alternative to traditional institution-based treatments in mental health, hospital, correctional and community-based settings (e.g. French *et al.* 1999).

Emergence of a recovery-oriented treatment system

In the evolution of the substance abuse treatment system, support has been inconsistent for recovery-oriented approaches in general and for TC programmes in particular. This reflects policy and ideological issues which underscore the need for new perspectives on treatment systems. Several of these issues are briefly cited.

Funding pressures have dramatically reduced the *planned duration of treatment*, often below threshold levels of time needed for stable change. This policy contradicts the science documenting the relationship between retention and outcomes in both community and correctional TC studies.

The contemporary call for evidence-based *strategies* has focused upon treating specific behaviours such as drug use. This contrasts with evidence-based *programmes* such as TCs which are multi-interventional approaches designed to address the multidimensional 'disorder of the whole person'. Despite considerable research documenting the effectiveness of these programmes, policy makers and scientists still do not fully accept the TC as a cost-effective treatment approach.

Finally, the *fidelity* of TC programmes has declined in part as a reaction to these various issues. Efforts to shorten programme duration to treat serious abusers engenders less favourable outcomes; the incorporation of various evidence-based strategies (e.g. CBT or MET), while useful, has substituted for rather than enhanced the active ingredient of the TC, *community as method.*

Managing disease versus promoting recovery

More broadly, the existing system of treatment for serious substance abusers, which has evolved to address the diversity of substance abusers, is not guided by what is known about the disorder and about recovery. Its focus on addiction as a chronic relapsing disease and on harm reduction has under-emphasized initiatives to promote long-term recovery.

Although useful from a public health perspective, a chronic-relapsing disease perspective implies that addiction cannot be overcome. However, the extensive research, including natural history and long-term treatment follow-up studies, underscores a more appropriate message: addiction is a chronic (recurring) disorder from which many individuals can and do recover. Thus, an enlightened treatment system is one that is grounded in promoting recovery and not simply managing disease.

The recent decade has witnessed a re-emergence of the concept of recovery in discussions of substance abuse treatment policy (e.g. White, Boyle and Loveland 2003; White, Kurtz and Sanders 2006). This has been accompanied by increasing attention to the issue of system change to accommodate the diversity of clients, problems and the chronic nature of the disorder. These themes are most evident for substance abusers treated in correctional settings who require a systems approach to facilitate their re-entry into society (Centre on Evidence-Based Interventions for Crime and Addiction (CEICA) 2007).

What is known about recovery from research and clinical experience in TCs can inform the rationale, objectives and activities of an effective treatment system. Stable recovery from addiction requires sobriety but includes broad changes in behaviours, cognitions, emotions and values.

As a continuing and developmental process of change, recovery requires a sufficient time in treatment as an initial goal. For example, completion of long-term treatment in TCs prepares the individual to continue in a self-change process which is reflected in impressive recovery rates years after treatment. These TC concepts offer insights for developing systems of continuity of care, which are integrated to sustain the individual in the recovery process. The last section of the chapter briefly illustrates key elements of a recovery-oriented system.

A recovery-oriented integrated system: A case illustration

A recovery-oriented integrated system (ROIS) model for correctional populations, as conceptualized by De Leon and colleagues (De Leon 2007), consists of treatment interventions, social services and surveillance activities guided by a common perspective on the substance abuse disorder and recovery. The goals of re-entry and recovery are mutually pursued in various settings including prison-based TCs, correctional transitional centres, community-based halfway houses and in the community at large. The main components of a ROIS approach consist of a recovery stage framework and a system-wide recovery management capability. A recovery stage framework is a general formulation of recovery as a change process which informs assessments and placements for the client in the system. It profiles where clients are in recovery and suggests what they need to facilitate further movement in the recovery process (see Table 5.1).

Table 5.1 A ten-stage recovery paradigm

Early stages	
Denial	Active abuse and/or associated problems, with no problem recognition or problem acceptance
Ambivalence	Some problem recognition, but inconsistent acceptance of the consequences of continued use on self and others
Motivation (extrinsic)	Some recognition and acceptance of drug use and associated problems, but attributed to external influences and not seen as reasons for seeking change
Motivation (intrinsic)	Acceptance of drug use and associated problems, and an expressed desire to change based on positive and negative inner reasons
Readiness for change	Willingness to seek change options which are not treatment related (superficial attempts)
Readiness for treatment	Rejection of all other options for change except treatment

Table 5.1 A ten-stage recovery paradigm *cont.*

Middle stages	
Deaddiction	Detachment from active drug use; pharmacological, behavioural and social detoxification
Abstinence	Stabilized drug freedom for a continuous period, usually beyond the individual's longest period of drug freedom
Late stages	
Continuance	Sobriety plus personal resolve to acquire or maintain the behaviour, attitudes and values associated with the drug-free lifestyle
Integration and identity change	The interrelation of treatment influences, recovery stage experiences and broader life experiences resulting in self-perceived change in social and personal identity

Source: Abbreviated from De Leon 1996

A system-wide recovery management capability refers to the collection of key correctional and community-based stakeholders organized as partners to facilitate the continued recovery of the client. Partners utilize a common framework for recovery, maximize communication and co-operation in the linkage activities across settings and they establish common assessment tools and procedures for evaluating and tracking client progress through the system.

An illustration of the ROIS model currently in development in correctional settings is more fully described elsewhere (De Leon 2007). Briefly, ROIS clients move in small peer cadres through a continuum of settings, a prison-based TC, a TC-oriented corrections-based transitional centre, a TC-oriented post-release residential halfway house, followed by parole supervision and ambulatory treatment in the community. In each setting, the goals of re-entry and recovery are mutually pursued. Treatment interventions, social services and surveillance activities are guided by a common perspective on the disorder and on recovery. Thus, it is continuity of perspective (*recovery*), method (*TC-oriented*) *and* community (*peer relationships*) which constitute an integrated system of care.

Conclusion

The TC is a recovery-oriented treatment pathway, which can inform the development of a recovery-oriented treatment system. The feasibility of implementing the ROIS model for correctional populations has been demonstrated but its effectiveness in promoting long-term recoveries remains to be empirically evaluated. Nevertheless, the face validity of the model has implications for substance abuse populations in general.

References

Centre on Evidence-Based Interventions for Crime and Addiction (CEICA) (2007) *Implementing Evidence-Based Drug Treatment in Criminal Justice Settings. Final Conference Report*. Philadelphia, PA: Treatment Research Institute at the University of Pennsylvania.

De Leon, G. (1984) *The Therapeutic Community: Study of Effectiveness*. National Institute on Drug Abuse Treatment Research Monograph Series (DHHS Publication No. ADM 84-1286). Rockville, MD: National Institute on Drug Abuse.

De Leon, G. (1996) 'Integrative recovery: A stage paradigm.' *Substance Abuse 17*, 51–63.

De Leon, G. (1997) (ed.) *Community as Method: Therapeutic Communities for Special Populations and Special Settings*. Westport, CT: Greenwood Press.

De Leon, G. (1999) 'Therapeutic Communities: Research and Applications.' In M.D. Glantz and C.R. Hartel (eds) *Drug Abuse: Origins and Interventions*. Washington, DC: American Psychological Association.

De Leon, G. (2000) *The Therapeutic Community: Theory, Model, and Method*. New York: Springer Publishing Company.

De Leon, G. (2007) 'Toward a recovery oriented integrated system.' *Offender Substance Abuse Report 11*, 6, 81–88.

De Leon, G. (2008) 'Therapeutic Communities.' In M. Galanter and H.D. Kleber (eds) *The American Psychiatric Publishing Textbook of Substance Abuse*, 4th edn. Washington, DC: American Psychiatric Publishing, Inc.

Ernst & Young (1996) *Review of Long Term Residential Treatment for People with Alcohol and Other Drug Use Problems*. National Drug Strategy, Commonwealth Department of Human Services and Health.

French, M.T., Sacks, S., De Leon, G., Staines, G. and McKendrick, K. (1999) 'Modified therapeutic community for mentally ill chemical abusers: Outcomes and costs.' *Evaluation and the Health Professions 22*, 60–85.

French, M.T., Salome, H.J., Krupski, A., McKay, J.R., Donovan, D.M., McLellan, A.T. and Durell, J. (2000) 'Benefit-cost analysis of residential and outpatient addiction treatment in the State of Washington.' *Evaluation Review 24*, 609–634.

Griffith, J.D., Hiller, M.L., Knight, K. and Simpson, D.D. (1999) 'A cost effectiveness analysis of in prison therapeutic community treatment and risk classification.' *Prison Journal 79*, 352–359.

Harwood, H.J., Foundation, D. and Livermore, G. (1998) *The Economic Costs of Drug and Alcohol Abuse in the U.S. – 1992*. Rockville, MA: National Institute on Drug Abuse and National Institute of Alcohol Abuse and Alcoholism (NIH 98-4327).

Harwood, H.J., Hubbard, R.L., Collins, J.J. and Rachal, J.V. (1988) *The Costs of Crime and the Benefits of Drug Abuse Treatment: A Cost Benefit Analysis Using TOPS Data*. NIDA Research Monograph 86, 209–235.

Harwood, H.J., Hubbard, R.L., Collins, J.J. and Rachal, J.V. (1994) 'The costs of crime and the benefit of drug abuse treatment: A cost benefit analysis using TOPS data.' In C.G. Leukenfeld and F.M. Tims (eds) *Compulsory Treatment for Drug Abuse*. Rockville, MA: National Institute on Drug Abuse (NIH 94-3713).

Lees, J., Manning, N. and Rawlings, B. (2004) 'A culture of enquiry: Research evidence and the therapeutic community.' *Psychiatric Quarterly 75*, 279–294.

Lipton, D.S., Pearson, F.S., Cleland, C.M. and Yee, D. (2002) 'The Effects of Therapeutic Communities and Milieu Therapy on Recidivism: Meta-Analytic Findings from the Correctional Drug Abuse Treatment Effectiveness (CDATE) Study.' In J. McGuire (ed.) *Offender Rehabilitation and Treatment: Effective Programmes and Policies to Reduce Re-Offending.* Chichester: John Wiley & Sons.

McGeary, K.A., French, M.T., Sacks, S., McKendrick, K. and De Leon, G. (2000) 'Service use and cost by mentally ill chemical abusers: Differences by retention in a therapeutic community.' *Journal of Substance Abuse 11*, 265–279.

Mitchell, O., Wilson, D.B. and MacKenzie, D.L. (2006) *The Effectiveness of Incarceration-Based Drug Treatment on Criminal Behavior.* Campbell Collaboration Systematic Review. Available at www.campbellcollaboration.org/lib/download/98, accessed September 2009.

Pearson, F.S. and Lipton, D.S. (1999) 'A meta-analytic review of corrections-based treatments for drug abuse.' *Prison Journal 79,* 4, 384–410.

Smith, L.A., Gates, S. and Foxcroft, D. (2006) *Therapeutic Communities for Substance Related Disorder.* Cochrane Database of Systematic Reviews 1, CD005338.

White, W., Boyle, M. and Loveland, D. (2003) 'Recovery management: Transcending the limitations of addiction treatment.' *Behavioral Health Management 23*, 33–34.

White, W., Kurtz, E. and Sanders, M. (2006) *Recovery Management.* Chicago, IL: Great Lakes Technology Transfer Center.

CHAPTER 6

NW ROIS: Recovery-Oriented Integrated Systems in North West England

Mark Gilman and Rowdy Yates

Introduction

Over the last four decades in England there have been four organizing principles for investing in drug treatment. In the 1960s and 1970s the very minimal investment that was made in drug treatment services simply sought to improve the life chances of the relatively small number of *individuals* with a substance misuse disorder (MacGregor 1989; Turner 1994; Yates 2002). In the 1980s investment was increased in services that sought to improve *public health* by protecting the public from the high-risk behaviours of a larger number of injecting drug addicts (Berridge 1994, 1996). In the 1990s and into the 2000s even more investment has been made to improve *public safety* by providing substitute medication-based treatments to heroin addicts to reduce crime (Bean 2002; Stimson 2000; Yates 2000).

Public expenditure on drug and alcohol treatment is notoriously difficult to estimate and expenditure within the private sector is effectively unknown. The UK Government, in its annual report to the European Monitoring Centre for Drugs and Drugs Addiction (Eaton *et al.* 2008), estimates 'labelled' expenditure for 2007/8 at a little under £1 billion. However, this figure is calculated using the United Nations Classification of Functions of Government (COFOG) and excludes a number of significant funding streams. Similarly, the UK Government's most recent strategy document (HM Government 2008), *Drugs: Protecting Families and Communities*, estimates 'labelled' expenditure at £958 million for 2009/10 but notes that around £1.2 billion will be spent in related areas. A more extensive calculation of Scottish public sector expenditure on alcohol and drugs has been undertaken by Audit Scotland (2009). This estimates total expenditure at £173 million with around 68% of this being invested in treatment services. For the UK as a whole, the Royal Society of the Arts (RSA) (2006) has estimated that the percentage of total 'labelled' expenditure allocated to treatment hovers around 38–40%, whilst the percentage for research and evaluation is less than 1%.

Whatever the true costs of UK public spending in addiction treatment services, it would appear undeniable that significant funding is being invested and that this funding has increased dramatically in the past two decades (Ashton 2008). What remains to be clarified though is whether the returns on this investment are being maximized. Audit Scotland (2009), in a comprehensive survey of public expenditure on addiction treatment, complained about the complexity and variability of the funding streams and questioned whether this was the most efficient way to deliver vital services. The RSA (2007), in a major report entitled *Drugs – Facing Facts*, noted that the 'gold standard' of core services surrounded by a seamless array of 'wraparound' services was both rarely available and, to some extent, devalued the non-clinical (wraparound) services by implying that they were peripheral and of less importance. De Leon, in a detailed propositional paper describing his recovery-oriented integrated systems (ROIS) approach,[1] noted: 'A poorly coordinated and conceptually unrelated system leads to duplication or lack of services, non-utilisation or poor utilisation of services, cost inefficiency, and often wasteful professional and agency turf conflicts' (De Leon 2007, p.82).

The organizing principle for investment in treatment interventions in the UK is shifting towards the '3 Rs' of *Recovery, Reintegration* and *Regeneration*. The potential benefits and outcomes of a ROIS are significant. A model of drug treatment delivery that focuses on the clinical and medical management of addiction seeks to address mortality and criminality. In so doing the orthodox medical treatment system satisfies the basics of the therapeutic alliance between professional and patient: keep the person with a substance use disorder alive and out of prison.

---

1   For a detailed description of the ROIS approach, see De Leon, Chapter 5 in this volume.

A ROIS approach seeks to go beyond the clinical and medical basics. ROIS seeks to get people with substance-use disorders into employment, training and education and able to look after their own children. Thus ROIS has the potential to deliver psychosocial outcomes that are commensurate with the level of investment. This is a crucial factor as the UK wrestles with the worldwide economic downturn. In fact, the economic downturn and economic recovery is analogous to individual and community recovery from substance misuse disorders. Eventually the economy will hit a 'rock bottom' and start to recover. The same process occurs in individuals, families and communities. The problem with treatment systems that focus exclusively on the clinical and the medical is that people do not recover as quickly, nor as comprehensively, as they would in a ROIS. Treatment systems with a narrow medicalized focus will often conceptualize their interventions around a definition of substance misuse disorders as 'chronic and relapsing conditions'. Numerous authorities from Weisman (1973) to McLellan et al. (2000) to White and McLellan (2008) have characterized addiction in this way, but much of the thrust of their arguments has been widely misinterpreted. White makes this point more clearly in later publications (White 2008). The intention was not to characterize addiction as 'incurable' but to shift the focus of treatment away from a narrow model of acute care towards a longer-term recovery management perspective.

This recurring belief in the irreversibility of addiction tends to breed an air of therapeutic pessimism that spreads from professional to patient and back to other patients. In these systems, professionals and patients grow old together. Apart from relapses into street drug use, there is little observable change in the patient from one year to the next. Methadone maintenance treatment (MMT) can go on for life. There are people who live full and productive lives on MMT. There are also many others for whom MMT is part and parcel of surviving against a backdrop of social exclusion, alcohol misuse and welfare dependence. This reality has been recognized and characterized as 'methadone, wine and welfare' (Preble and Casey 1969). Too often the legitimate prescription of a substitute drug appears merely to offer the opportunity for a 'safety net' to soothe the highs and lows of an unpredictable supply of illegitimate street drugs (Best and Ridge 2003). The National Treatment Agency for Substance Abuse[2] (NTA 2007) reported that less than 30% of methadone-prescribed

2 The National Treatment Agency is a special health authority within the National Health Service (NHS), charged with the responsibility to improve addiction service provision and quality in England.

clients claimed *not* to have used other illicit substances. Of those who admitted 'topping up', 82% admitted to having used heroin. Similarly, the Drug Outcome Research in Scotland (DORIS) study found that 67% of drug users on an MMT programme admitted to having used heroin (Bloor *et al.* 2008).

The development of ROIS in the North West of England began in 2005 when the NTA launched its 'treatment effectiveness strategy' (Dale-Perera 2005). The treatment effectiveness strategy signalled a shift from a focus on *quantity* (getting more people into treatment quickly) to a focus on *quality* (retaining people in treatment for at least 12 weeks and then getting them out of treatment and back into mainstream society). The NTA's constituency is made up of three groups: *commissioners* of drug treatment, *providers* of drug treatment and *users* of drug treatment, and equal importance is afforded to each of these stakeholder groupings.

Commissioners

Treatment service funding is administered at all three levels of English Government. There are 150 local authorities or councils spread across nine English regions. The nine Government Offices for the regions report to Central Government in Whitehall. This administrative arrangement means that treatment service priorities, delivered at the local level, will be determined by commissioners in the local areas. These commissioners are organized around partnerships, generally known as Drug and Alcohol Action Teams (DAATs). The engine room of the DAAT is the Joint Commissioning Group (JCG). This is a much smaller group, representing individual and pubic health interests, criminal justice and children and families departments. Prior to the development of the ROIS agenda it was often difficult to engage with the most senior people in these organizations. The ROIS initiative is beginning to attract executive level interest because of the potential of ROIS to address some of the key issues of social exclusion: worklessness, looked after children and the intergenerational transmission of substance misuse disorders.

When the NTA launched the treatment effectiveness strategy in 2005, the North West region began a recovery pilot. This began with the specific aim of increasing access to abstinence-based treatments. The North West had relied very heavily on MMT. Following an initial meeting in Manchester in June 2005 it soon became clear that what was missing in the North West was not abstinence. Rather, the missing link was a recovery orientation to treatment. The next stage involved contacting the real experts in this: the recovered or recovering people themselves. White (2009) and others have noted that this 'recovery community' represents an extensive, largely untapped resource which, for the most part, has remained hidden from mainstream treatment providers and planners. How had these groups and individuals recovered? How had many of them moved from the margins of society into employment (addressing worklessness) and become responsible parents (preventing the state from having to look after their children)? It soon became clear that people do recover from substance misuse disorders. If this is a chronic and relapsing condition then it is one that many, many people recover from. Moreover, recovery delivers people who will go to work and look after their children. Recovery also appears to have the ability to create a firewall in the intergenerational transmission of addiction.

On 3 August 2005 we were invited to address the Public Service Board in Blackburn with Darwen, a small unitary authority in Lancashire. The Public Service Board, or Local Strategic Partnership, is the most important and influential partnership in any of the 150 English Local Authorities. At this meeting, it became clear that the existing treatment network was seriously flawed. If the drug treatment system in Blackburn with Darwen was to contribute to the council's key strategic aims, it had to change. In essence it had to develop a recovery orientation. The treatment services had to integrate with each other and the commissioners had to create and manage a ROIS.

We have since found a much more useful model to emulate. The City of Philadelphia in the USA has undergone something of a revolution in the transformation of their treatment system towards a recovery-oriented system of care (White 2009). Representatives from North West England have visited and established good links with colleagues in Philadelphia and other US cities. Commissioners in England had become used to using Models of Care (NTA 2006) as a proxy national service framework and as a 'shopping list' against which to purchase services. This experience has not helped them in commissioning a ROIS.

A ROIS cannot be purchased 'off the peg'. It requires the commissioner to act as the architect of a revised and modernized system. The commissioning of a ROIS also requires vision, leadership skills and the courage to resist those whose vested interests a ROIS challenges. Courage is also required when facing those services that cannot, or will not, work within the ROIS model. The ROIS must involve both communities of geography and communities of interest. The Wired In online recovery community (http://wiredin.org.uk) has proved extremely useful as a rallying point for those in the process of commissioning, providing and experiencing a ROIS. In time the ROIS will benefit from recovery centres and even 'recovery villages' run for community members by community members.

Recovery centres and recovery villages will be able to provide employment, training and education for the most vulnerable in the economic downturn. Commissioners need to set goals whereby the community of services in a ROIS is able to demonstrate how they can keep someone actively engaged for two years to increase the chances of positive outcomes. That said, a ROIS understands lapse and relapse as the rule not the exception. Commissioners can be the most powerful and important change agents. They can use the process of re-tendering and market testing to introduce ROIS. For example, commissioners can insist that traditional medical services (e.g. large NHS Mental Health Trusts) bid for contracts in partnership with organizations with a proven track record in delivering recovery outcomes. It is through active commissioning that the 'integration' element of the ROIS can be introduced and managed (De Leon 2007). Commissioners can require existing providers to integrate with other providers in the community of services. Inter-agency referrals can be monitored quarter by quarter and repeated failure to integrate with other services would thus become legitimate cause for re-tendering and market testing.

Providers

Once commissioners have decided that they want to create a ROIS they need to speak to their current providers. The most important and influential providers are those who receive the majority of funding for the provision of MMT and other substitution medication-based maintenance treatments. Obviously, there have been some issues to work through with these providers in the development of a ROIS. Some partnership areas have tried to work with their existing providers in the construction of a ROIS. Others have decided to decommission existing services and have gone to the market place to find providers with a track record of producing recovery outcomes. As there are so few existing recovery-oriented community treatment providers, many established (MMT) provider services have had to forge partnerships with them in order to secure business. Decommissioning existing services and going to the market place is probably the swiftest and most effective way for commissioners to create a ROIS. It is very difficult to motivate existing maintenance-oriented services to embrace recovery (Day *et al.* 2005). In those areas where this has been tried, there have been very few, if any, referrals from the maintenance services to recovery options. Of course, it is entirely possible that existing maintenance treatment providers could win contracts once they have made the necessary partnership arrangements with a recovery-oriented treatment service.

One of the biggest challenges facing existing providers is the attitude of many of their staff towards recovery. Many have never seen anyone recover and so they can be very cynical and sceptical (Yates *et al.* 2005). Many of them suffer from contempt prior to investigation and need to understand, accept and 'adjust' their own treatment prejudices: 'There is a principle which is a bar against all information, which is proof against all arguments and which cannot fail to keep you in everlasting ignorance – that principle is contempt prior to investigation' (Spencer 2002, p.23).[3]

Much of this can be overcome by in-house training. All staff can be trained in recovery principles and practice. The starting point for many will be to gain an understanding of 12-step programmes and 12-step mutual aid. Attendance at open meetings of Narcotics Anonymous (NA), Cocaine Anonymous (CA) and Alcoholics Anonymous (AA) should be a requirement of all staff including managers. There is also much to be learnt by utilizing the International Treatment Effectiveness Project's (ITEP) node link maps and mapping.[4] There are also some very practical changes to be made. For example, if your service provides MMT does it adequately facilitate 'medication-assisted recovery'? Can people be in treatment with your service and still be in employment? Does your service open at times that are accessible by people in full-time work? Or are the service's policies, practices and opening times governed by the assumption that most patients will be unemployed and on welfare and therefore able to attend the service in office hours?

It is crucial that staff in all treatment services within a ROIS matrix are aware of the parts played in the ROIS by other services. In practical

---

3   This quotation, by the English philosopher and sociologist, is well known within the 12-step recovery community from its use in the *Big Book* – the Alcoholics Anonymous 'manual'.

4   The ITEP was a joint initiative between the NTA and the Institute of Behavioral Research (IBR), Texas Christian University. The IBR website contains much useful information (www.ibr.tcu.edu/info/nwitep.html). A summary report by the NTA is also available (Campbell *et al.* 2007).

terms this will often require the commissioners to be prepared to remind some professionals that they (the commissioners) are in charge because they (the commissioners) hold the money and invest that money in the system for the good of individuals and the community at large. The most common tension in UK treatment systems is between commissioners, the medical profession and psychiatry. This tension is easily overcome if the commissioners make judicious use of re-tendering and market testing.

Users

There are many challenges facing service users in a ROIS that are not apparent in a traditional medical management system. The most fundamental challenge arises when the ROIS informs the client that they must take responsibility for their own treatment journey. We often hear the slogan, 'treatment works'. However, the caveat, which should always be added, with respect to recovery-oriented interventions, is that, 'it works best if you make it work for you' (Broekaert 2002; White 2008).

Substitute prescribing and problem management approaches can work with or without the client's active engagement and there is, for example, a long tradition of using depo-injections for the administration of anti-psychotic medications. As long as the patient takes their methadone the state should get its crime reduction dividend and deaths should be prevented – keeping people alive and out of prison. Recovery, however, will only ever happen when the patient or client becomes actively involved in driving forward his or her own treatment plan. Recovery happens when the patient or client takes control of their treatment journey and the professionals assist. That is, when the patient is 'on top' and the professional is 'on tap' (McKnight 2000). This is one of the biggest challenges to the creation of ROIS in the UK. The growth of treatment in the UK has been amongst people on the margins of society. MMT has become a feature of life in the most disenfranchised and disadvantaged communities (Shaw, Egan and Gillespie 2007).

The orthodox medical management of substance use disorders has a tendency to infantilize service users and discourages them from taking control of their treatment and their recovery. This tendency manifests itself most clearly when people ask to be directed towards abstinence-oriented recovery and are told that they 'are not ready' (Yates *et al.* 2005). In the eyes of the infantilizing professionals they are 'not ready' because abstinence-oriented recovery is 'too dangerous' (Ashton 2008;

Gibson and Degenhardt 2005). In one swift, well-intentioned move, the service user's motivation to change is squashed by a risk-averse professional concerned primarily to prevent overdose (keep them alive). These attitudes have seen many service users opt out of orthodox treatment to take their chances with 12-step mutual aid in the form of NA, CA or AA. Many others have started their recovery journey whilst in prison. At the time of writing, there are very few people in recovery who got there via orthodox (Tier 3) maintenance treatment services. The development of ROIS has also seen a schism emerge in service user involvement circles. When the NTA was established, most of the service user groups were made up of people in MMT. Their primary concerns revolved around prescribing issues: what substitute drugs were available or not, in what preparations and for how long was observed daily pick-up imposed. With the establishment of ROIS, service users have become much more interested in identifying routes and roads to recovery. This interest is heightened every time a former service user finds recovery and spreads the message back to current service users via attraction not promotion.

For many service users, recovery was an abstract and alien concept until one of their own peer group found recovery and came back to show others the way. Once an area has a critical mass of ex-service users in recovery the prospect of an indigenous recovery community becomes a distinct possibility as opposed to a wild dream.

12-step mutual aid

There are many forms of recovery support. Self Management And Recovery Training (SMART) and Intuitive Recovery are two recent additions and welcome options for people recovering from substance use disorders. Therapeutic communities, too, have continued to promote notions of a holistic recovery within a self-help framework, although they have been largely marginalized during the past two decades (Yates 2003). There is likely to be an increasing role for faith-based organizations that are already engaging with marginalized groups and communities. However, it is 12-step mutual aid fellowship groups that seem best placed and most likely to form the nucleus of any recovery community. A clear indicator of a successful ROIS will be the number of local meetings of NA, CA and AA in the operational area. In this context, Liverpool and the Merseyside area have seen unprecedented growth over recent years.

Summary

The North West recovery pilot began in the summer of 2005 and formally ended on 13 November 2008. The development of ROIS is now spreading out from the North West of England to the rest of the UK. There is a point in the development of any movement or organization – and the recovery-oriented integrated systems of care initiative is no different in this respect – when a 'tipping point' is reached (Gladwell 2001). The recovery tipping point has been reached in the North West of England. Those professional groups and organizations opposed to recovery will find it very difficult if not impossible to halt the march of recovery. People who have the misfortune to experience a substance use disorder do recover. They have been recovering in their thousands and millions ever since Bill Wilson decided to head to the phone booth rather than the bar in the Mayflower hotel in 1935. Those in recovery and those who have recovered are the experts and it is by their power of example that generations to come will recover from substance use disorders. Recovery-oriented integrated systems of care will ensure that commissioned professional treatment assists this process and that professionals remember that their place is to be 'on tap' not 'on top' (Kretzmann and McKnight 1998).

References

Ashton, M. (2008) 'The new abstentionists.' *Druglink* (Special Insert), Dec/Jan 2008.

Audit Scotland (2009) *Drug and Alcohol Services in Scotland.* Edinburgh: Audit Scotland.

Bean, P. (2002) *Drugs and Crime.* Cullompton: Willan Publishing.

Berridge, V. (1994) 'AIDS and British drug policy: history repeats itself...?' In R. Coomber (ed.) *Drugs and Drug Use in Society: A Critical Reader.* Greenwich: University Press.

Berridge, V. (1996) *AIDS in the U.K.: The Making of Policy 1981–1994.* Oxford: Oxford University Press.

Best, D. and Ridge, G. (2003) 'Using on Top and the Problems It Brings: Additional Drug Use by Methadone Treatment Patients.' In G. Tober and J. Strang (eds) *Methadone Matters: Evolving Community Methadone Treatment of Opiate Addiction.* London: Martin Dunitz.

Bloor, M., Mckintosh, J., McKeganey, N. and Robertson, M. (2008). '"Topping up" methadone: An analysis of patterns of heroin use amongst a treatment sample of Scottish drug users.' *Public Health 122,* 1013–1019.

Broekaert, E., Vandevelde, S., Vanderplasschen, W., Soyez, V. and Poppe, A. (2002) 'Two decades of "research-practice" encounters in the development of European therapeutic communities for substance abusers.' *Nordic Journal of Psychiatry 56,* 5, 371–377.

Campbell, A., Finch, E., Brotchie, J. and Davis, P. (2007) *The International Treatment Effectiveness Project.* London: National Treatment Agency.

Dale-Perera, A. (2005) *Improving Drug Treatment Effectiveness.* Briefing for launch on 30 June 2005. London: National Treatment Agency.

Day, E., Gaston, R., Furlong, E., Murali, V. and Coppello, A. (2005) 'United Kingdom substance misuse treatment workers' attitudes toward 12-step self-help groups.' *Journal of Substance Abuse Treatment 29*, 321–327.

De Leon, G. (2007) 'Toward a recovery oriented integrated system.' *Offender Substance Abuse Report 11*, 6, 81–88.

Eaton, G., Davies, C., English, L., Lodwick, A., McVeigh, J. and Bellis, M. (2008) *United Kingdom Focal Point Report 2008*. Lisbon: UK Focal Point/EMCDDA.

Gibson, A. and Degenhardt, L. (2005) *Mortality Related to Naltrexone in the Treatment of Opioid Dependence: A Comparative Analysis*. Sydney: National Drug and Alcohol Research Centre.

Gladwell, M. (2001) *The Tipping Point*. London: Little, Brown Book Group.

HM Government (2008) *Drugs: Protecting Families and Communities*. London: HMSO.

Kretzmann, J. and McKnight, J. (1998) *Building Communities from the Inside Out: A Path Toward Finding and Mobilizing a Community's Assets*. Skokie, IL: ACTA Publications.

MacGregor, S. (1989) *Drugs and British Society: Responses to a Social Problem in the 1980s*. London: Routledge.

McKnight, J.L. (2000) 'Rationale for a Community Approach to Health Improvement.' In T. Bruce and S. McKane (eds) *Community-Based Public Health: A Partnership Model*. Washington, DC: American Public Health Association.

McLellan, A.T., Lewis, D.C., O'Brien, C.P. and Kleber, H.D. (2000) 'Drug dependence, a chronic medical illness: Implications for treatment, insurance, and outcomes evaluation.' *Journal of the American Medical Association 284*, 1689–1695.

National Treatment Agency for Substance Misuse (NTA) (2006) *Models of Care for Treatment of Adult Drug Misusers: Update 2006*. London: National Treatment Agency for Substance Misuse.

National Treatment Agency for Substance Misuse (NTA) (2007) *Harm Reduction Findings from the NTA's 2006 Survey of User Satisfaction in England*. London: National Treatment Agency for Substance Misuse.

Preble, E. and Casey, J.J. (1969) 'Taking care of business: The heroin user's life on the street.' *International Journal of the Addictions 4*, 1, 1–24.

Royal Society of the Arts (2006) *The Economic Impact of Illegal Drug Use (Discussion Document)*. London: RSA.

Royal Society of the Arts (2007) *Drugs – Facing Facts*. London: RSA.

Shaw, A., Egan, J. and Gillespie, M. (2007) *Drugs and Poverty: A Literature Review*. Glasgow: SDF/SAADAT.

Spencer, H. (2002) *Principles of Biology*, vol. I. Seattle, WA: University Press of the Pacific.

Stimson, G. (2000) 'Blair declares war: The unhealthy state of British drug policy.' *International Journal of Drug Policy 11*, 4, 259–264.

Turner, D. (1994) 'The Development of the Voluntary Sector, No Further Need for Pioneers?' In J. Strang and M. Gossop (eds) *Heroin Addiction and Drug Policy: The British System – Volume 1*. Oxford: Oxford University Press.

Weisman, M. (1973) 'The Para-professional in a Medical Setting.' In G.E. Staub and L.N. Kent (eds) *The Para-professional in the Treatment of Alcoholism*. Springfield, IL: Charles C. Thomas.

White, W. (2008) *Recovery Management and Recovery-Oriented Systems of Care: Scientific Rationale and Promising Practices*. Philadelphia, PA: North East Addiction Technology Transfer Centre/Great Lakes Addiction Technology Transfer Centre/Philadelphia Department of Behavioral Health & Mental Retardation Services.

White, W. (2009) *Peer Based Addiction Recovery Support: History, Theory, Practice and Scientific Evaluation*. Philadelphia, PA: Great Lakes Addiction Technology Transfer Centre/Philadelphia Department of Behavioral Health & Mental Retardation Services.

White, W. and McLellan, A.T. (2008) 'Addiction as a chronic disease: Key messages for clients, families and referral sources.' *Counselor 9*, 3, 24–33.

Yates, R. (2000) 'On trial for association: An examination of the relationship between drugs and crime.' *4th European Conference on Rehabilitation and Drug Policy, February 22–26, 1999.* Marbella: PlanMarbella/EFTC, 311–316.

Yates, R. (2002) 'A brief history of British drug policy, 1950–2001.' *Drugs, Education, Prevention and Policy 9,* 2, 113–124.

Yates, R. (2003) 'A brief moment of glory: The impact of the therapeutic community movement on drug treatment systems in the UK.' *International Journal of Social Welfare 12,* 3, 239–243.

Yates, R., McIvor, G., Eley, S., Malloch, M. and Barnsdale, L. (2005) 'Coercion in Drug Treatment: The Impact on Motivation, Aspiration and Outcome.' In M. Pedersen, V. Segraeus and M. Hellman (eds) *Evidence Based Practice – Challenges in Substance Abuse Treatment: Proceedings of the 7th International Symposium on Substance Treatment, November 25–27, 2004, Aarhus.* Helsinki: Nordic Council for Alcohol and Drug Research/University of Aarhus/EWODOR/EFTC.

CHAPTER 7

The Therapeutic Community as a Method of Intervention

Wendy Dawson and Albert Zandvoort

In this chapter we provide a brief overview of the concepts underlying the therapeutic community (TC) for addictions, link these to the actual experience of the Ley Community, an addiction TC based in Oxfordshire, England, and include the story of a former resident. Finally we will discuss some challenges with regard to the further development of TCs within the UK.

Addiction TCs in the UK are less common than TCs focusing on enduring mental health difficulties, a situation which differs from most other areas of the world, particularly the US, Latin America, Europe and some parts of Asia. The term 'therapeutic community' often means a residential treatment facility for drug and alcohol treatment. Therefore, most of the research on addiction TCs comes from these areas.

Research (Brook and Whitehead 1980; De Leon 2000; National Institute on Drug Abuse (NIDA) 2009; Ravndal 2001; Rawlings 2001) and on-site visits by the authors, to treatment facilities in the US and Europe, indicates that the concept of the TC for the treatment of addictions in many cases offers improved long-term results when compared to other treatment modalities. The research indicates that residents who successfully completed their long-term treatment had higher levels of sobriety and lower levels of criminal behaviour. More were in gainful employment and showed lower levels of depression than prior to treatment.

The TC for the treatment of addictions can be defined as follows:

A therapeutic community is a drug-free environment in which people with addictive (and other) problems live together in an organized and structured way in order to promote change and make possible a drug-free life in the outside society. The therapeutic community forms a miniature society in which residents, and staff in the role of facilitators, fulfil distinctive roles and adhere to clear rules, all designed to promote the transitional process of the residents. Self-help and mutual help are pillars of the therapeutic process in which the resident is the protagonist principally responsible for achieving personal growth, realizing a more meaningful and responsible life, and upholding the welfare of the community. The program is voluntary in that the resident will not be held in the program by force or against his/her will. (Ottenberg, Broekaert and Kooyman 1993, p.52)

The TC approach to addictions views the problem as a disorder of the whole person, which affects the physical, emotional and spiritual well-being of the individual and the family. In particular, substance misuse is seen as a symptom of underlying difficulties and as an over-learned behaviour functioning as a coping strategy in the face of life's harsh realities (Perfas 2003). The goal of the TC approach is to facilitate growth as defined above, rather than as to be seen as, for example, a conventional 28-day treatment programme.

Often TCs define themselves not through specific methods or programme elements, but rather through common shared values which underlie all aspects of their work. For instance, the Royal College of Psychiatrists in the UK manages a 'Community of Communities' project for which they have published a set of 15 core standards (Community of Communities 2007) which forms the basis for their accreditation of TCs. Below are a few of these core standards:

- The whole community meets regularly.

- All community members work alongside each other on day-to-day tasks.

- Community members take a variety of roles and levels of responsibility.

- All community members regularly examine their attitudes and feelings towards each other.

- All community members create an emotionally safe environment for the work of the community.

De Leon (2000) also identified certain key assumptions that characterize a TC belief system, the first being the belief that a TC approach is effective, followed by the belief that the community-as-method approach facilitates change. This approach is a social learning process, where residents learn from observing each other and themselves. Importantly, the TC as a community, rather than a single therapist or counsellor, is the healing force that facilitates individual change. Residents assume responsibility for their behaviour and they are deemed to be able to change and become responsible members of mainstream society (Kooyman 1993).

Perfas (2003, p.129) adds the following: 'The belief in the inherent goodness of man' – residents are not judged by their past, but by what they do in the here and now to correct their mistakes – and the belief in helping another person help themselves, i.e. the willingness to 'go the extra mile' to support a fellow resident. These assumptions also underpin the approach of the Ley Community, which as previously stated, is an addiction TC, accredited by the 'Community of Communities'.

The Ley Community approach

The Ley Community is a not-for-profit independent registered charity in Oxfordshire, UK. It was established in 1971 by two local psychiatrists, Dr Bertram Mandelbrote and Dr Peter Agulnik. In 1969 Dr Agulnik visited Phoenix House in New York and was so impressed by the impact of the Phoenix self-help programme and its emphasis on ex-addicts in treatment helping each other with their recovery that he decided to implement this model in the UK. The two pioneers recruited John McCabe, an ex-Phoenix House graduate from New York, as programme director to develop the Ley Community further as a dedicated addiction TC.

The Ley Community approach can be summarized as a combination of 'tough love' and 'self-help'. The 12-month programme provides a framework for residents to learn from each other and change the way they have behaved, thought and felt over many, many years. Building positive relationships with other residents is central. The programme allows residents a chance to come to terms with themselves, and to enhance their self-confidence and self-esteem. This all takes place within a climate of safety, which means that residents are no longer threatened from outside and there is no exposure to drugs of any kind. At the same time, the culture of 'unconditional positive regard' (Rogers 1978) and mutual respect allows every resident to feel accepted.

A common language is used to help bond staff members and residents and ensure that everyone understands and reinforces the same concepts and practices. The community that is established in the Ley TC functions as a facilitator of change. The community's structure creates a family-like atmosphere, conducive to psychological, behavioural and social change.

In terms of 'rational authority' professional clinical staff members have the authority to make all decisions related to residents, including status, discipline, promotion, transfer, discharge, furlough and treatment planning. Staff members use this authority in a consistent, trustworthy, compassionate and rational way and clearly explain the reasons for their decisions.

A daily routine is strictly followed. All residents are given responsibilities within a clearly defined structure. The structure encourages planning and serves to delay the impulse for immediate gratification. As residents progress in their recovery, the level of responsibility increases with more senior residents supervising the work of junior residents. Senior residents are also responsible for promoting the TC culture and represent the role models who have successfully managed their change process and can now stimulate growth in the younger members.

Therapy groups provide an opportunity to examine behaviour, attitudes and values in the context of day-to-day problems. Through this process, residents come to understand themselves better, gradually assume personal responsibility and begin to establish trust in one another. Alongside the work and therapy, residents are encouraged to participate in educational opportunities, voluntary work and recreational activities. As residents grow, it becomes increasingly important to allow them to make individual choices in line with their increased sense of responsibility for themselves and the community – and ultimately the wider community into which they will be integrating.

The Ley Community therapeutic programme

The programme is structured into three phases:

Phase 1: Orientation, primary care and main therapeutic intervention

This phase usually lasts six months and intervention is focused on three levels of presenting issues.

COGNITIVE AND BEHAVIOUR ISSUES

New residents typically have poor judgement and poor awareness of themselves or of how their actions affect themselves and others, and they also experience difficulty in decision making and in problem solving. They usually do not see themselves as worthy people or as valuable members of society, have low self-esteem and often see themselves as social deviants or victims of society.

EMOTIONAL ISSUES

New residents have difficulty identifying and talking about their feelings, in restraining themselves from emotional outbursts or aggressive behaviour and are less able to tolerate frustration or emotional discomfort. They also experience a great deal of guilt or shame.

SOCIAL ISSUES

New residents often have no drug-free friends and have possibly engaged in criminal activities. Mostly they are disengaged from mainstream culture and society. In the early stages of this phase residents are encouraged to 'act as if', which means they behave like the person they should be, rather than the person they have been (De Leon 2000).

Phase 2: Move on and resettlement

In this phase residents use the 'tools' learnt from the main therapy phase as they re-engage within the wider society through voluntary or paid work together with being 'supervised' by more senior residents who are in the final stage of this phase in work but are still living in the community. This two-stage process usually consists of two periods of three months each.

Phase 3: Aftercare

Residents are living independently and in full-time work. They are supported by the Aftercare Team who respond to 'early' and 'crisis intervention' as part of relapse prevention and who provide a weekly 'drop in' at a local community centre where there is the opportunity to touch base with peers, seek advice and guidance on all aspects of living drug- and/or alcohol-free or simply to have a chat. Aftercare support is provided for up to one year and longer if needed.

Graduation

Following reintegration into mainstream society and having been successfully 'clean' for over one year post discharge, ex-residents are invited back to participate in a graduation ceremony – a prestige ceremony to mark their rite of passage and to receive a silver ring embossed with the Ley Community emblem in recognition of their achievements.

In summary, the Ley Community residential programme promotes motivational change as described in teaching-module 3 of *Introduction to the Therapeutic Community Curriculum* (Substance Abuse and Mental Health Services Administration (SAMHSA) 2006) through:

- behaviour management and behaviour shaping by engaging residents in a learning process that involves developing prosocial behaviour and rewarding positive behaviour

- enhancement of emotional and psychological life by providing a supportive environment in which residents can explore feelings, help each other identify recurring destructive patterns of behaviour and experience personal growth

- improvement of work and vocational skills by emphasizing the work ethic and independent living skills so that residents can be self-supporting and contribute to society after they leave the TC

- enhancement of intellectual and spiritual life as residents are encouraged to grow by thinking through their problems and learning about a world greater than themselves.

In many therapeutic communities, including the Ley Community, spirituality is not necessarily part of the design. Perfas (2003, p.126) defines spirituality as 'any action or activity that reflects and brings out the goodness of man'.

It has been the experience of the authors that during the recovery phase, spirituality often is the addict's response to the existential emptiness that has characterized most of their life. Having lived a life that was mostly devoted to the selfish pursuit of personal gratification, accompanied by feelings of guilt and shame, many addicts embrace a larger ideal, which may include a religious belief, when they finally embark into a life of sobriety.

Challenges to the therapeutic community concept

The challenges to the therapeutic community methodology are:

- Commissioning – there is less and less 'spot and block' purchase from procurement officials, which means that TCs have to be on a preferred supplier list, which does not guarantee fast access to our service and generally reduces our throughput. The commissioning of mental health-related services in the UK tends to be a maze, even for insiders and suppliers who have dealt with the National Health Service for many years. It is hoped that the new initiative towards world-class commissioning will alleviate this situation.

- The UK Government still sets targets which encourage and support the maintenance of addicts on methadone prescriptions in order to stabilize and reduce illicit drug use figures. In our view this policy does not enable addicts to recover since it often closes the door to alternative and more successful treatment pathways like TCs.

- In the UK the focus is generally on drug misuse being firmly fixed within the criminal justice system rather than being seen and treated as a health issue. Again, this leads to people not having timeous access to the services they require.

- Procurement officials show a clear lack of understanding of a treatment programme that delivers a long-term solution to addiction through an intensive and constructive method of intervention over 12 months. There is a clear preference in the UK for short-term programmes, which do not deliver the same good results.

- Street-level agency staff tend to be inexperienced and target driven rather than being focused on the long-term recovery needs of the addict.

- And, finally, the UK has a prison system which favours methadone maintenance and which shows a clear lack of signposting into treatment programmes based on abstinence.

Case study: Trudy's story
My life before coming to the Ley Community

Before coming to the Ley Community rehabilitation centre, I had been offered rehab several times and decided to go to jail instead, as I liked smoking drugs.

I first went to jail for importation; I got an eight-year sentence and went to Holloway. At the time I was very scared and could not see the light for looking. In Holloway I discovered heroin; it was a great time killer on a 23-hour Bang Up. Since my eight-year sentence, I have done six years for the same thing and about four years for robbery, not to mention a good few remands.

I was well and truly just another statistic in the system. This vicious circle needed to be broken. I was stuck in my ways and had very little understanding of myself.

Coming to the Ley

As if by accident, I came to the Ley, and on my day placement I swore I would not be back. As far as I was concerned, no one here had a clue what I was going through. I worried about so many men being around me and what they might think about me and my past. I didn't really know what to expect, as I only knew what I had heard on a day placement. Although I say I came here by accident, the truth is I did really hand my life over, as I could no longer cope with it. I needed to get away from my hectic lifestyle.

When I was in jail, rehab was never mentioned. I was given methadone and put on a few drug courses where they tell you the harm each drug does to you. No one encouraged me to sort myself out. If you don't know about such things, you really don't know where to go with it.

At detox, I was simply too ill to move. Even though my body had shut down, my mind wouldn't rest. When I came here, I was rough. I felt that it was just another institution with rules, like any other jail but without the bars. I kept telling myself it's like jail, to cope better. The change was hard for me, everybody wanting me to see what they saw in me and how I made people feel around me.

I felt that I was not liked and I was misunderstood. I thought people were picking on me. Most of all, I felt like a child again, having to learn new ways of dealing with things (my anger and feelings) but I am getting there slowly.

My life at the Ley

This is my understanding now: I have always wanted what I wanted, when I wanted it. I hated the word no and acted on impulse, like most junkies. It was my way or the High Way. When I came here, I had a jail attitude and nasty defences. The Ley has slowed that right down and I have learned more about myself then I thought possible. I have learned more about myself by being in this programme, than I had in 30 years.

I have learned to treat people as you would like to be treated yourself. It is important for me to treat people with respect, as they treat me. The Ley has showed me that if you work for something, you can get it. If you are true to the game, it will be true to you. By that, I don't mean I take this as a game, far from it. I actually like myself now. I no longer look at residents as men or women; they are people like me with drug problems. Out there, a lot of people gave up on me. Now, people believe in me and that makes me want to do my best. It is a good feeling.

The Ley is not a bad place; the key is staying here and facing your fears without drugs. It is not about addressing your drug use; it is about your attitude and behaviour problems: 'Why do we do what we do?' and 'What can we do to change?' I am not in jail; these people are not my jailers. I am free to go. I hate to say I was wrong before, but I was very wrong. No harm can come to you. I would definitely recommend this place, as jail never taught anyone anything. Rehab can help you change the way you think and behave.

My future

My future looks brighter then ever. The greatest opportunity the Ley has given me is getting my life back. I have hope that maybe I can do this and I will stay drug-free and get a job. It has given me the chance to meet people who I will do the programme with. Those people are real friends with no hidden agendas and no secrets. Everything is on the table.

I would not get those simple little things out there, where I've got nothing but associates for a smoke, rape, robbery and a hectic life-style. One is one too many and a thousand is never enough.

References

Brook, R.C. and Whitehead, P.C. (1980) *Drug-free Therapeutic Community*. New York: Human Sciences Press.

Community of Communities (2007) *Service Standards for Addiction Therapeutic Communities*. London: Royal College of Psychiatrists.

De Leon, G. (2000) *The Therapeutic Community: Theory, Model and Method*. New York: Springer.

Kooyman, M. (1993) *The Therapeutic Community for Addicts: Intimacy, Parent Involvement and Treatment Success*. Amsterdam: Swets & Zeitlinger.

National Institute on Drug Abuse (NIDA) (2009) *Therapeutic Community*. NIDA Research Series 12. Rockville, MD: NIDA. Available at www.drugabuse.gov/ResearchReports/Therapeutic/default.html (accessed 5 September 2009).

Ottenberg, D., Broekaert, E. and Kooyman, M. (1993) 'What Cannot Be Changed in a Therapeutic Community?' In E. Broekaert and G. Van Hove (eds) *Special Education Ghent 2: Therapeutic Communities*. Ghent: vzw OOBC.

Perfas, F.B. (2003) *Therapeutic Community: A Practice Guide*. New York: iUniverse Inc.

Ravndal, E. (2001) 'An Outcome Study of a Therapeutic Community Based in the Community: A Five Year Prospective Study of Drug Abusers in Norway.' In B. Rawlings and R. Yates (eds) *Therapeutic Communities for the Treatment of Drug Users*. London: Jessica Kingsley Publishers.

Rawlings, B. (2001) 'Evaluative Research in Therapeutic Communities.' In B. Rawlings and R. Yates (eds) *Therapeutic Communities for the Treatment of Drug Users*. London: Jessica Kingsley Publishers.

Rogers, C. (1978) *On Personal Power*. London: Constable.

Substance Abuse and Mental Health Services Administration (SAMHSA) (2006) *Introduction to the Therapeutic Community Curriculum*. Rockville, MD: SAMHSA.

CHAPTER 8

Voices of Recovery

David Bryce, Carl Edwards,
Maggie and Annemarie W.

David Bryce, *Calton Athletic Recovery Group, Glasgow*

David Bryce is the founder of Calton Athletic Recovery Group (CARG) which he set up in the East End of Glasgow in 1985 as a football team and support group for recovering addicts. CARG supports young men, from the local area and beyond, in their recovery from alcohol and drug addiction. The project combines personal and group support, with physical activities such as football, fitness training and other activities which provide an alternative way of life to many of the young men who approach the project for help. Despite the success of CARG in getting the young men straight and sober, and supporting them to stay that way, the project has struggled for funding and is currently without any resources from the statutory sector. David's book *Alive and Kicking* (with Simon Pia) was published by Mainstream Publishing in 2005.

Interviewer (INT) What does recovery mean to you?
David   Recovery means abstinence from drugs and alcohol; after all alcohol is the oldest drug known to man. And through my experience I have discovered that alcohol is the starting point and the finishing point of a relapse, so recovery means being drug- and alcohol-free. And it also means it's not enough to stop, or to put the cork in the bottle. Recovery means change; rehabilitation; to restore to one's former self; one's former self

doesn't include prescriptions from the chemist or alcohol. My former self was brought up without drugs and alcohol – going back to that is what I take to be rehabilitation; it's not enough to be abstinent, you have to have a willingness to change. That's what recovery is about.

INT   *How would you describe your own experience of recovery?*

David My experience was sort of haphazard – trial and error, but it resulted in abstinence from alcohol and from drugs. Unfortunately I was put on a methadone prescription and I realize, with the benefit of hindsight, that I didn't start recovering until I had put down the methadone and withdrawn from it. And that's when I started to recover. At that time, there were no services about to speak of. There were no residential units, there were no community projects; the only thing that really helped me properly was going to Alcoholics Anonymous (AA). I got identification with the alcohol side of it, no problems with that. I think they helped me in a way that no other people could at that time. You could certainly empathize with the people that were sober and it was something that I wanted, a bit of contentment, a bit of happiness in my life.

I was demented because the drugs had robbed me of everything and given me nothing in return. By that I mean my character, my abilities, my physical strengths, it robbed me of everything and left me with an empty shell. However, I discovered that the meetings weren't enough for me. I had no social skills, and I had to develop social skills. I had no hobbies; I had to get interested in things because what I did discover, through trial and error, was that if I had no contentment or no happiness in my life I wasn't going to succeed with my recovery. I was going to fail at one point or another, so that's the way it was for me, trial and error. And we (CARG) tried to develop a programme for others that was simple in nature but effective, in effect a simple programme for complicated people, addicts and alcoholics can complicate anything.

INT   *Can you say a bit about how your programme differs from other approaches?*

David   What I learnt from my own experience was invaluable. But it wasn't much good for putting character back into my life; to do that I had to do character-building activities. Once I discovered the therapeutic values of that, combined with the knowledge that I got from AA, I had a good mixture to begin with. When you are left with an empty shell you need to start to achieve things. Things started to come into my life, like running – which I started when I came off the drugs and the booze. Up till then I couldn't eat a Marathon (chocolate bar) never mind participate in a marathon and actually finish it! I hated running, but I have got an awful lot of running medals now because the thing I hated did me an awful lot of good when I was doing it. And it isn't really rocket science, but I didn't know then that scientifically when you use drugs, particularly heroin, your body stops producing a natural substance called endorphins because the heroin does the job for it. So by the time you stop using heroin the body has forgotten how to produce endorphins, and the only way it learns is when you start to push the body, i.e. through running or physical activities which produce a feeling of well-being. I know that's endorphins today, I didn't know it then, and that's part of the trial and error process.

Some things were good for me; some things were bad for me. Things that were bad for me were going out and trying to socialize at dance halls with people who were drinking and still using drugs. That was terrible for me. I was ignorant and I think I wanted to show everybody that I could do it. Today I am big enough to admit that was probably the biggest threat to my recovery, me thinking I was impressing people when I wasn't. I was just making it hard for myself; that's all part of the trials and tribulations that we went through to perfect this programme that we have got today.

Learning how to make it easy – that's the simple programme for complicated people. Simple things like going to weddings, funerals, christenings – 97% of social gatherings involve alcohol. And I discovered through experience that when I put myself in a situation where alcohol was about I started to feel uneasy. I realized I was feeling uneasy because I am a recovering alcoholic and I will be for the rest of my life. Once I accepted that, things started to get easier. I started to make it easier for myself; I started to make it easier for people following behind me. They don't have to make the same mistakes; some people are prepared to take on board what you are telling them. Other people have to find out for themselves but when they find out for themselves it maybe reinforces the message that we were right from the start.

Even the workplace was hard. You are working with people who are all looking forward to Friday night fever, and they are talking about it and you maybe think you are missing out on things. Learning how to cope with that situation is important and of course, there are certain employments more susceptible to the booze than others. But again it's all a learning process. I really discovered how immature I was when I stopped using the booze and the drugs. I don't think I had developed these things when I started drinking as a 14-year-old and I didn't get them until I stopped when I was 27. I was an immature boy as a 27-year-old, I didn't know how to be a father, didn't know about responsibilities, I was ignorant, really ignorant. I discovered that, and really recovery is about growing up, development, realizing your future is in front of you not behind you.

INT   *You mentioned that you still saw recovery as ongoing; you described yourself as a recovering alcoholic. Do you see that as something that continues throughout the rest of your life?*

David   Yeah and I'm proud of it. At one time it was a daunting thought; this is what I have got to do for the rest of my life, because at that time I wasn't particularly happy. The cork was on the bottle; all my previous experience had either been full of drugs or full of booze, so I was a very depressed guy and I thought I was going to be depressed for the rest of my life. It made it a bit easier when I accepted it was only for a day at a time and I might not be depressed tomorrow, especially if I do something positive about myself today. You know – having the ability to change things. And I have no doubt that after 33 years, if I picked a drink up it would take me to the exact same places that it took me 33 years ago. I don't need to find that out by doing it, I have worked with too many people all around about us trying it, and I have not seen any of them succeeding; every one of them went down, some of them quicker than others.

INT   *You mentioned that you felt your recovery started when you had got off the methadone, was that the point where you think that you started to recover?*

David   Yeah. The methadone was the last link to the drugs. I realize with the benefit of hindsight all I did was delay my withdrawals for six weeks; nobody told me I would have to withdraw off the methadone which I had to do. That withdrawal was the exact same withdrawal I had after heroin, if anything a bit worse because withdrawals don't get better they get worse. The one clear advantage I probably had over everybody else was that I had already stopped drinking five years beforehand. So alcohol was never part of my recovery from drugs. And I think that's how I sustained it and other people didn't. They couldn't accept they were drug addicts and that included alcohol – they thought it was only powdered drugs, or drugs from the corner, or from the chemist that were the problem. They didn't have the knowledge that I did that alcohol was the oldest drug known to man. It's still the most destructive drug probably known to man and it does more damage in this country than any other drug. So that was the one advantage I had, I had accepted from day one when I came off the methadone that alcohol wasn't going to be part of my recovery. I made it when hundreds of thousands of people around about me didn't make it. Maybe they were looking for easier, softer options; I already knew that alcohol wasn't going to be part of recovery. I had already made a mess of my life through alcohol and I had to watch many other people making a mess of their life through alcohol after coming off illegal drugs. It's almost as if they wanted to hold on to a bit of the corner. Alcohol was socially acceptable, so people coming off would find they were maybe even encouraged by their parents to go out for a drink: 'stay away from these dirty drugs, come out for a drink with us'. Then after a couple of drinks it became a good idea for the individual to go and get a gram of something else because no matter who you are, your inhibitions come down once you have got a couple of drinks in you. And what was a bad idea to start with suddenly becomes a good idea through the alcohol. So now the people who come to Calton Athletic are told to stay away from the alcohol. There weren't many examples at that time, except myself, I was abstinent from alcohol when we started implementing it. That's when quality really got introduced to Calton Athletic, maybe about three or four years into its development.

I am no different from anybody else who has had a spiritual awakening; in the early days I thought I could cure the world and help everybody, and I had to get real through experience, and realize the only people I could help were people who were prepared to help themselves. I learnt through experience that people that wanted to drink could go somewhere else and drink, because what I did become aware of is the bad apple effect. If you have got somebody drinking, or using, and you don't deal with it, that will affect other people around about that are trying harder. When I walked into meetings years ago and there were people using I wasn't listening to what the speaker was saying, I was too busy looking at the people that were using and I discovered I am not unique in that. I realized that there is only so far you can go in trying to help everybody by making allowances. It's preventing people from getting to recovery, and once we implemented the requirement of abstinence from alcohol that's when we started to achieve things, particularly the ability to go places as a group and be ambassadors. In the past when we went to places and people were drinking, inevitably the ones who were drinking caused disruption and we didn't get invited back. If they are sober they are manageable, if they are drinking they are uncontrollable, it's that simple; it's not rocket science. But it has been difficult getting people to accept that is what it's all about. And I think they really accept it when you can do it by the power of example. It isn't enough that Davie is sober; everybody else at Calton is sober. They are all doing well and the reason why they are doing well is because they are sober. If people want to drink again in their life, they can go somewhere else and some of them end up coming back to us, and that has happened to a lot of people. They couldn't accept that recovery from alcohol is for the rest of their life. After a few years they tried it and found themselves back in the same situation. I know that, because they came back to the organization. Not everybody can manage it on the first attempt. Some people have to learn by their mistakes and it's not a problem for us when they come back. When they do, we don't have to teach them the rules. They know the rules, they learned them the last time, maybe at that time they just couldn't accept the rules.

INT   *What do you think are the most helpful factors in getting somebody to the point of recovery and sustaining it?*

David   Sustaining it is the important thing. When I was serious about it, I wanted to be in amongst other people that were serious and determined. I was prepared to go to any lengths to achieve that. And I think other people have got to go to any lengths to achieve it, but the best way I can help them is to try and make sure the organization is full of people that are serious about their recovery. There are different ages here: 50-year-olds, 40-year-olds, 30-year-olds, 20-year-olds, a good mixture of age and experience. They have all got a good sense of humour; they might not have had that good sense of humour when they came through the door, because I think drugs rob of you that as well, you have got to learn to laugh again. But the serious side of Calton Athletic is the power of example, everybody providing a service in the organization is sober and drug-free, it's as simple as that. Not everybody in Calton Athletic provides a service, but to do so in Calton Athletic you have to be sober and drug-free for a year. The quality of members has improved year upon year. At one time we were happy doing the West Highland Way, then a couple of boys went on the Inca trail. Through their example, everybody thinks they can do the Inca trail and maybe even Everest, because that's what it's about, not about resting on your laurels.

At one time we just had the football team who played once a week with no training; now the football team has got to train. They don't just compete, they win things because that's what winners do – if you are a winner, you win things. And when we were out there and we were using, we all considered ourselves losers, but now we are winners. We set standards and goals, and those goals and standards are there to be beaten. The football team that nobody gave a hope in hell of lasting a season went on to win the Scottish Cup twice. To me that's equivalent to Berwick Rangers winning the Champions League – nobody would give them a hope in hell, nobody gave us a hope in hell. And it's the same with the marathons; at one time it was enough to get around it. Now we are looking for good times when we are doing it; people want to do better and that's human nature.

INT   *Can I ask what you mean by members providing a service?*

David   Helping other people and helping the wider community. I believe when you start to provide a service it's like an apprenticeship. It takes you time to learn things. The first thing that people get involved in is on the education side. We provide a structured programme and we go into the schools, and try and explain in an hour and a half how easy it is to get started on drugs. We talk about the lifestyle you have got to maintain once you become addicted and the people that you affect through your addiction. We find this is kind of thought provoking and encourage the audience to ask any question they like. And in effect we are trying to demystify everything that is out there about drugs. Usually the information young people get about drugs is from their friends, and they discover when it's too late that they don't know as much as us. Young people might know the prices and the pleasant effects of the drugs but nobody tells them about the realities of drugs. And that's what we do in the schools, and probably that's the first stage in the ladder in the provision of services, providing a service in the schools.

    Somebody that has got several years of quality time under their belt might move on to become an individual counsellor. By that point, they would have gone through a process of training at the club and watched the whole process from start to finish – people coming through the door, people getting detoxed, people going into rehabilitation, and aftercare, and they would have the ability to support somebody during that process. Things haven't changed in the 30 years or so since I have been in recovery. There was no magic detox, there was no rehab when push came to shove and when I came off, I had to go through withdrawals in the house. And probably 95% of the people coming through Calton Athletic have had to follow a similar route. Everybody speaks about the horrendous withdrawal; that's the easy part but you don't discover that until you are down the road. That only lasts for five days, the mental part lasts a lot longer: depression, the mood swings, you are looking good but feeling depressed. People don't understand that, but somebody that's been through it can empathize with the psychological effects after you have put the drugs down. That's the hard bit; almost everybody that's addicted to drugs goes through withdrawal at one time or another, voluntarily or involuntarily.

It's a bit harder now because at one time when you went to jail you were forced to go through your withdrawals. Now when you get the jail they can maintain your habit. Residential rehabs are becoming respite centres and people are being supported with drugs while they are in there. And other agencies are actually speaking about recovery while their clients are still on drugs. That's not recovery to me. That's not recovery to the wider community out there. Just because you are getting your drugs at the chemist doesn't mean you are recovering.

INT   *One of the things the government strategy talks about is this idea of communities of recovery and it seems to me that you have created a community of recovery here by the support that you provide to the guys, and the guys provide to each other.*

David   Well that's exactly what we are – a community in recovery. We don't all stay up the one close, or in one street, obviously we are based in the East End and the bulk of the people coming through the door are from the East End. But I am proud to say that they are not exclusively from the East End. There are boys from the north of the city, the south and the west. It's probably easier to get here if you are in the East End and you know somebody at Calton Athletic.

People tell me that the hardest thing is having to walk through the door at Calton Athletic for the first time. And these guys aren't wimps, some of these are tough boys, and it's the fear of the unknown, about what it is going to be like when they walk through the door. Once they walk through the door they discover that these are groundless fears, but nevertheless these groundless fears can keep people away. And in fact misconceptions have kept people away: that we only want people that are good at football; we only want guys from the East End. Some think we only want Protestants but the reality is that it doesn't matter whether someone is Catholic or Protestant, black or white, anybody is accepted through the doors at Calton Athletic as long as they have got a willingness to be abstinent and a willingness to start to change.

The first thing they get at Calton Athletic is hope that it can be done. Then they start to get inspired by the people around about them. It's as simple as that and it is a community, it's a sober community, and it works. We have had 4000 people through the door at Calton Athletic and it worked when we had no resources. It made it better when we got resources because we could open up to more people. When we stopped having resources it still worked and if anything it maybe worked better, but certainly, for a fewer amount of people. It works better because the people at Calton Athletic have got more quality, more experience, and more time under their belt and that's what it is about.

In terms of providing a service, I don't think there is a course anyone can take that will make them a good counsellor; it's like an apprenticeship – it takes time. You have to learn it, and you need hands-on experience. Calton Athletic judges people on their ability not their qualifications. I have seen many people with qualifications who were horrendous at providing a service, and I have seen people with no qualifications who could become the best in the business, through hard work and experience. Sometimes it's about being unpopular; it's about telling people what they have to hear not what they want to hear. Anybody can tell a person what they want to hear – that's not going to get them better. It's telling them what they have to hear, and it's about being cruel to be kind as well. That's probably the main reason the quality of Calton Athletic has increased year upon year, having that ability to get rid of the bad apple and realizing through experience what that bad apple can do.

We need to realize that qualifications are about experience – when I got involved in this game there were no qualifications for this kind of work. The only qualification I had was experience; I was fortunate that somebody gave me the opportunity to do something because of my life experience. Somebody gave me the opportunity; I am in a position to give other people that opportunity. And I am a good judge of who will make it in this line of work and who will not make it because you have got to have basic attributes to start with. Life experience isn't enough; there have got to be other commodities in your life as well: like being a good communicator; having the ability to lead by example; being a good listener; telling people what they have to hear not what they want to hear. And showing people that recovery is there to be enjoyed, not endured.

INT   *What do you think should be the way forward with the agenda on recovery?*

David   The way forward is to make it easy for people to get to Calton Athletic; obviously given the number of people who come to the club means that we need resources to deliver the service. If we had the resources, we could reconstruct the services more or less immediately. Calton Athletic has changed beyond belief; we started off with the football team, and we are still very proud of it. But the reality is nearly everybody coming through the door at Calton Athletic will not play for the team, they aren't good enough for the team. But they will all be involved in something physical and it's not just about resources, it's about having the support of government as well. That's so important. We are not doing this for ourselves, we are doing it for the people of Scotland. The government represent the people of Scotland; thankfully we have got a new government with a new strategy. But it's easy to talk about a strategy; I am convinced the people that are managing the drug problem, mainly the Drug and Alcohol Action Teams, have no intention of implementing the strategy. They are still speaking about people that are on methadone as being in recovery. And I am afraid that's what their idea is for the Road to Recovery. People on methadone get more opportunities than people that are prepared to come off drugs. That's the real problem you know, people aren't getting rewarded for coming off drugs, they are being rewarded for staying on drugs. By rewarded I mean they get extra benefits, they get prioritized for housing, their kids will get childcare, they will be offered all sorts of employment, all sorts of training. People shouldn't be penalized for taking another way out; with threats that they will get taken off benefits, by having to find their own houses, having to find their own jobs, and everything else. That's what has happened to us over the years. In effect it's actually probably produced more quality here, we have got people that can find their own jobs, that are prepared to make sacrifices to move forward.

What is not right is that a lot of people can't move forward because of the financial implications. It costs the guys money to get to Calton Athletic, members have to pay to come here and help other people. We like to see people as many days a week as possible but it costs money. The gym costs money, the marathons...everything costs money. Nobody here gets anything for nothing, maybe rightly so but we should be able to assist and help them. Not every family has got the financial clout to help out and what I have discovered and still maintain is that we don't deal with a transient lot of homeless helpless people from bad families. The people that come to us are from decent families, hard-working families. The main problem in their family's life and their own life is their addictions. And that's what we tackle first; the statutory agencies seem to have it in reverse. They tackle everything bar the addiction and achieve nothing because how can you look after a house when you have lost control? And that's what addiction means, to lose control, so they are asking people to control themselves who can't do it because they are addicted. It maybe sounds good in theory but it certainly doesn't work in practice. And an old timer like me from the Gallowgate with no university degree could spot 15 years ago that that policy was fatally flawed. And it is even more of a problem to give an addict drugs and tell them to control it. If they could do that they wouldn't be addicts in the first place. So it sounds good in theory but it's been a disaster in practice.

There have been record numbers of deaths, year upon year, and infection has spread out of control. There are more prostitutes on the street than ever before, so all this money is really producing nothing except more of the same and this problem is affecting the wider community. There is probably no bigger a killer in the drugs field than alcohol and methadone together. And as the recent alcohol report showed this goes beyond alcoholic deaths: it's not just the alcoholic poison, it's the violence; it's the carnage on the roads, and everything else. And that's what I am now seeing in the drugs field; most of the people that have died with drugs aren't dying with needles sticking out of their arms. They are dying from complications of hepatitis C, cirrhosis of the liver, asphyxia; it's just never ending and it's not going to end.

INT   *Do you think that the new strategy has changed anything or offers a potential for change?*

David   No, for us it has not changed anything because obviously we haven't got any funding and we just have what we had before which is nothing. But really we have been more successful with nothing than many others have been with a lot of funding. We can show tangible results from our efforts, people off the drugs, off the alcohol, not offending, being productive, back at work, being good parents, or good sons and daughters, or ODCs, Ordinary Decent Citizens. That's the goal at Calton Athletic to be ordinary decent citizens, maybe more than ordinary decent citizens, maybe outstanding citizens in some cases.

But at the end of the day what has been happening all along is that the resources are being put into managing the drug problem with people still using drugs. They have been trying to perpetuate a myth that people going on methadone were in recovery. People that are on methadone are practising drug addicts; methadone is a class A drug, very addictive, a very dangerous drug, and somehow they think they are off the drugs. Nothing seems to be changing except we have now got an industry built around about them that is spending more money than ever and producing more deaths than ever, more kids needing to be taken into care than ever, and infection out of control.

INT   *You mentioned that you have had to struggle for funding and resources in the past, and that situation is continuing now. Do you think you present a challenge to other agencies?*

David   Of course it presents a challenge because I am not a professional but I am more professional than many of them at this game. Being a professional means being good at your job, probably getting paid – and that's where I am not professional. I don't get paid to do what I am doing. There isn't a qualification to be a professional football player, all you have to be is good at it and be part of a team. I am good at what I do and I am part of a team at Calton Athletic. The best way forward is to help people to change their lifestyle and their attitude and you can't change it better than becoming abstinent and then you are into recovery. It's that simple. I heard that message 20-odd years ago and I have stuck to it and it works you know? And if you don't change your lifestyle and your attitude everything else is secondary; you are on your way to failure. If things weren't working at Calton Athletic we would put our hand up and try something else, and if certain things don't work or aren't cost effective we will switch to something else.

This is too insidious a disease. We are dealing with people that have lost the plot and we are trying to restore them to sanity. We, at Calton Athletic, recognized 20-odd years ago they were suffering from a mental illness that was progressive. The statutory funders, the statutory employees, are just starting to discover the true effects of the mental illness but it continues to manifest itself and all because we never pointed people on the true road to recovery. Not everybody has got the same expertise or the same experience, but with a willingness, we could all play a part by referring people to the appropriate agency, not just to an agency where funding has become available but might not be appropriate. We have certainly got a willingness to refer people to the appropriate agencies. If somebody comes to us and they are homeless for example, my expertise is not getting them a house, I could refer them to the agencies that are dealing with the homeless. Once they have solved their homeless problem they could be referred back to

Calton Athletic if they had a willingness to be abstinent and a willingness to change.

And I have laughed at other agencies which try to copy us, statutory funded ones which just put money into football – that is all pie in the sky. It's not going to succeed unless you tackle the main problem which requires abstention and working to deal with the addiction. That's why we have succeeded not just in the physical side, with the football, or the running, or the weight training; but we have got our own band now and we are very proud of that as well. It is about educating yourself in a new way of life, you don't learn that in a couple of weeks you know.

(Interview with Margaret S. Malloch)

Carl Edwards, *Parkview Project, Liverpool*

Carl Edwards is the founder of the 12-step residential project, Parkview Project. The project began when Carl purchased and restored a hard-to-let property in a deprived area as a sober-living house. Carl was also the instigator of the theatre and film company Genie in the Gutter.

INT   *What does recovery mean to you?*

Carl   First and foremost it means not being in the grip of addiction. To have that compulsion to use the thing that you know is killing you but you don't seem to be able at least to do anything about it. To have that removed, that's the mainstay of my recovery.

INT   *Is recovery being free of drugs and alcohol or just free of the drugs that were a problem for you?*

Carl   Alcohol ended up being my main drug if you like, my main drug of choice, and it also means not using the other substances I would use compulsively or that could lead me back to alcohol. For me it means not taking any mind altering substances and to live life on life's terms, to face all the challenges of the day without a chemical crutch. I think it's not so much a philosophy as an experience. I did try to modify things, I would not drink but I would say 'well OK I will smoke pot'. But I couldn't smoke pot recreationally. I would say 'well OK I won't drink but I am going to that wedding so I might have a couple of lines of coke' but I couldn't do that recreationally. So I would either become totally unsettled, totally ill at ease, feel as though the foundation that I was standing on was pulled from beneath my feet, and use those other crutches compulsively or it would take me back to drinking.

So it's not so much a philosophy it's just my experience. It seems like the only way forward for me really is to not have anything, because I just seem to end up in trouble if I try and take something else. So first and foremost it appears to me that I need to be abstinent. That doesn't mean that I wouldn't take something if the doctor prescribed it. If I was in severe pain and the doctor said I really needed to take co-codamol well then I would take it because I am not using it for the buzz, or to escape, I am using it for a real reason. Three months ago I ended up with stress from the job, and the three computers at work had low screens and the chair was high. I was crouching over them for the last couple of years working away and with the stress of the job I ended up with these terrible pains shooting up my neck and my back. So at one point I had to get an ambulance and go to hospital in the middle of the night.

I was in pure agony, I started to worry it was something else; the pains were really shooting up the back of my head. And I was off in an ambulance and the doctor gave me ten milligrams of diazepam and I took it and ended up on a course of diazepam for a week. But I took them for the right reasons. It was to loosen up these muscles. I ended up seeing a chiropractor and had to sort out the way I was sitting at the computers and generally chill out and relax. But on the third or fourth night I got into bed and I had taken the diazepam and I was beginning to look forward to them by this point after only a couple of days. And I said to my wife 'this pillow feels beautiful, oh these sheets…what have you done? Have you washed these sheets?' And she looked at me and she said 'you are off your head!' I felt all sort of wrapped up in cotton wool and the next day I got rid of them because the effect was really appealing to me. I was only taking a couple in the morning and then at night, but over the space of two or three days it went from pain management to thinking 'I like this' and that was without my permission.

But it did happen and I had to recognize that within myself and I threw them away, I did the chiropractor thing and went on to take some ibuprofen and co-codamol for another four or five days and it's been great since. I have altered all the computer screens so I am sitting directly opposite and it's been a lot better anyway. But it's just there, I just wonder if someone who hasn't had a problem with chemicals would have had that seductive type of feeling that I had.

And so I just think that if needs be you take something because the doctor says so, but I just feel as though I really need to be careful where chemicals are involved. So the first part of the answer to 'what is recovery?' For me it is to be abstinent of chemicals, in fact that's the baseline for me. People talk about working towards abstinence, I think abstinence is the first thing then you can work towards other things. That's my experience. I just seem to become vulnerable and I just lose my footing. I become preoccupied the minute I seem to take something. You know my whole mindset changes.

INT   *Are you saying that you think that you, and presumably other people with similar problems, have an addictive personality; or that when you are in recovery and you take something it sparks memories?*

Carl   I don't think it's like a recall thing in particular I think it's a right in the present experiential state. That effect of something which is very pleasing to me. Now why that is exactly, I don't know. I don't suppose I will ever know. People say 'oh you need to escape, take you away from yourself', well I don't know whether that's entirely true because I like being me. It's not like I really feel a need to not be me. So I have never understood that one. In fact sometimes I think it's the opposite, sometimes when I get high then I feel like I am myself.

INT   *I am curious to know was it like that the first time you used, did that feel like being you suddenly?*

Carl   Not then. No. Not with alcohol. I mean when I started I probably drank quite normally, other than being a bit of a dare devil alongside my peers, my friends. It was the bottles of cider before the disco on a Friday night when we were 14 and I was probably no different from them. At 16 I went away to sea and

I drank a lot less, alcohol just wasn't a thing, it wasn't an issue. I would have a drink or I wouldn't so it was gradual. There was a six-year period when my behaviour was a little bit strange two or three times. I was probably a bit over the top with alcohol. But there was certainly no issue or guilt or compulsivity or anything like that. The first time I got high on pot was probably the third or fourth time I had actually smoked it. I was a caterer at the time on the QEII, we were on a world cruise and we were pulling in to Rio de Janeiro and we were on the deck smoking pot and this was the first time it actually affected me. I don't know if it was the first time I inhaled it properly or what but a week or two leading up to that night I had had a few puffs and I hadn't felt anything. But that night I did and it was when the ship was actually pulling into Rio de Janeiro and I got high, I got really high and I remember looking at the statue of Christ up on Sugarloaf Mountain. And all of a sudden it was as if this religion just turned into a mythology right there and then. And I was high and I really enjoyed it very much. And the same happened with the class As, amphetamine, LSD, cocaine, from the minute I took them it was like 'this is what I want to do'.

I never graduated to heroin, I took heroin but I never got a habit so alcohol became my drug of choice in the end, but the obsession began with drugs not alcohol.

INT   *So what was the point when your recovery actually started, can you pinpoint that?*

Carl   Well I actually got sober on 1 August 1993 but I lived in the States and at some point during 1986 I actually said to myself that I must be an alcoholic.

At that point alcohol had become the main thing. I went to AA for a couple of weeks and I actually didn't drink for three weeks and then something happened, I can't remember what. But you could say it began then because a seed was planted. I was exposed to a way out of something, but it was actually seven years later I got sober. I was in and out of AA in Britain when I came back in 1988 but also in and out of hospital, dry outs, and that type of thing. So I don't know, maybe it started that day in 1986, but I do know at some point during 1986 I said 'I am an alcoholic'. It feels to me as though once I recognized that I had a problem maybe that's when it began. Others might say well it was when you actually stopped for good, but how can you say it's for good?

INT   *Did you just go to AA or was there more?*

Carl   No. There was something much more important than that I think. I went to AA on numerous occasions from 1988 to 1993 – there were four or five years where I was in and out, staying for a week, staying for days, whatever. But I hadn't made any changes within myself or around myself. I hadn't done what I really wanted to do – from the age of about 22 or 23 I had always wanted to go back to education. People who were educated fascinated me. I felt really inferior to people who were educated, I deeply wanted to do it. I wanted to be a well-read person. I wanted to do an English degree, I wanted to be a teacher, or a writer. In 1993 I was running a little fruit shop writing shit poems in the back of the fruit shop when I didn't have customers, which was most of the time, and drinking wine and smoking dope. So this time when I stopped drinking I closed the fruit shop forever. After a five-day detox I went and put my name down for GCSEs and so I changed something significant that was really important to me about my life. I did the GCSEs, well I finished half of them, and the next year I did an access course and over the next three years I did a degree, and over the next two years I did an MA. Education was really, really important. I don't think I would have stayed sober even in AA and NA (Narcotics Anonymous) if I had just opened the shop again because it wasn't me. I think what I am trying to say is, I had some authenticity about myself. I became more true to myself.

I made changes that reflected who I wanted to be, or thought I was.

INT   *Were there other things that supported your recovery at that time?*

Carl   Family. I had good family support. My mum and dad, and my brothers and sisters were at the end of their tether because we are a close-knit stable family. They were always there, they never left me, I live four miles away but I was up at their house every week. My self-esteem and my footing within the family grew.

INT *Were they actively involved in your recovery?*

Carl Oh yeah, my mum went to Al-Anon. And we would chat about things and my mum came to a meeting one time at AA. I suppose they were just actively involved in my life. One of the GCSEs I did was drama and we put a little show on, at the drama class and they would all come to that. I was encouraged. They weren't actively involved in any clinical stuff. Well there was no clinical stuff, I didn't go to rehab I just went to AA but they were actively involved in my life I would say. I think that was probably very important. There was also one other major change I made at that point, I had been obsessed with a woman down the road from this fruit shop, she is now dead, she died of alcoholism. She was an attractive woman in a very sexy way and we had a terrible stormy relationship. It wasn't even a relationship really, we were just drinking buddies. But she had a five-year-old son when we met. That week, 1 August 1993, I decided I wouldn't go back to her, that we would have nothing to do with each other any more. I stuck to my guns because I knew it was bad for me and for her, and I wouldn't stay sober if I was with her. But I kind of bonded with her son and he kept coming up to the house, we lived in the same street you see. And I would take him up to my parents on a Sunday and he refers to me now as his stepdad. So I have been actively involved in his life. I was the one who went up to the school and did this and that. I tried to bring him up right and I felt as though that gave me some responsibility and self-esteem. He has always been really important to me.

So what was important was not being with the woman I knew deep down I shouldn't be with for my sobriety, and helping Little Joseph, who is not little any more, he is 23. So in terms of family and relationships, there was my family and there were those two people as well.

INT *Tell me about how you started up Park View? How did that happen?*

Carl I finished the MA and it was the year 2000 and during the time I was doing the MA I had had a bit of a business in town.

A friend of mine and myself, we had four or five hot dog vans on the streets of Liverpool. And we made good cash you know but they wouldn't give us a licence and in the end they towed us away. But I had made some cash and there was a bunch of us in NA who had been talking about the fact that there was no rehab in Liverpool. 'Why is there no rehab, let's start a rehab!' It was just all talk…we would go to our meetings and then we would go to the café two or three times a week. Nothing ever got done and I had money and in 2002 I thought I would just spend it. I had been travelling and I went to Australia and I thought I would just end up spending it all. I didn't have a job, I needed a job. So I bought a 12-bedroomed house before the property boom and before they awarded the city the Capital of Culture. I got it cheaply and I had enough money to put a £5000 deposit down. My auntie was the chairman of the PCT (Primary Care Trust) over the water on the Wirral. And my brother had some cash, he had had some management experience so we formed a company and approached the DAT (Drug Action Teams). Eventually in May 2003 we formed a company. When it didn't look like we were going to get sufficient Supporting People funds and the DAT were still dithering, my aunt played it safe and took her money out and left. She subsequently emigrated to Australia and my brother played it safe too and took his money out. But then weeks later I had good news from the DAT and we were up and running.

So that was a 12-bed house and we slowly got a good reputation. There were people coming out of Park View and graduating and getting jobs as community drugs workers in Liverpool. We did a launch in May 2005 and there were a couple of hundred people there and I think people were impressed. We thought 'Bloody hell! This has taken off.' And I had just bought another property then, another 12-bed property, which we got for £80,000, and a year and a half later it was worth £300,000. It was fortuitous, I was lucky. And then the DAT supporting people came along and funded the second place, which became a secondary unit. It had two other nine-bed properties next door and next door but one to it which were dilapidated, and I bought them, got planning permission, knocked it all through, secured capital funding from the Strategic Health Authority via the NTA (National Treatment Agency). The NTA were right behind us, they loved it, Mark Gilman really loves this community rehab idea. I don't think it would have happened if it wasn't for him probably.

We have gone from strength to strength really. I have just bought the property next door to the one we started off at and I'm hoping the planning permission is going to go through in the next couple of weeks. We are going to knock through and turn what is now the secondary unit from 12 beds to 18 and I have just bought the property next door to that, it's not attached, its going to be a move on property. A move on place for people who have gone right through the programme, done the secondary work and so it won't be staffed it will just have floating support. We have just gone from strength to strength. The downside is the stress. I got into it, one to get a job and two because I really couldn't believe how the previous seven, or eight, nine years had gone. To be free of that bloody torment. And I wanted other people to get that, because it seemed to me that there was a whole perception out in Liverpool that you can't get well.

Well, I wanted people to know you bloody well can get well, and your kids can benefit from this. You can benefit from this, your family can benefit from this, it can be great. This is not a white-knuckle ride, it can be bloody good, you can enjoy your life. You can be who you are supposed to be.

INT	*Were there services that you avoided, that you wouldn't have gone to?*
Carl	No. There may well have been if I had been on heroin. In Liverpool we have a facility called the Windsor Clinic and that's basically the alcohol detox in Liverpool. They also do a three-week block after detox which runs on the philosophy of controlled drinking.

Now the first time I was in the Windsor Clinic in 1988 I had done the three-week block and I tried the controlled drinking. I went on to do the Windsor Clinic another three or four times for detox, and it's a really important facility for that, but I avoided the option of the controlled drinking because I knew it was just a waste of time for me.

INT *How important to your own recovery is it to be working in the recovery business?*

Carl At the time when we opened up I think it was very important. The first three or four years I felt the benefit of it, it was like a constant step 12, constant giving back. When I started, in the first few years, I was running groups and doing key working sessions and I was at the coal face, I had contact with clients. Now that's all gone, because we have expanded. It's good, more people have been helped, I am financially secure, but it's lost something as well. I can come in here some days now and I don't know who people are. I don't know their names; I have to ask staff 'what is that guy's name, what's this girl's name?' And there is something sad about it, and people have said 'look don't give yourself a hard time you are just doing what you are supposed to be doing, someone has got to do your job.' And I am not giving myself a hard time but some of the enjoyment has gone out of it you know. I don't know enough about the drug field on the strategy side of things. I have just basically set up and taken care of operations for seven years. I have never really sat back and been able to understand what is going on and the history, and who is who, and all the politics. So I can't really get myself fully into that because I am not experienced enough. But sitting in an office writing cheques and doing office-type stuff is not as fulfilling any more to be honest with you. And it can be stressful you know, ensuring quality and picking up all the loose ends and things. But I really did feel positive the first few years working with people. I really did feel the benefit of that. I mean it was nothing new because I had done that in AA and NA for quite some time. I had always tried to help but it was good though, it really was.

I know the frontline people are experiencing that now. A lot of our staff really enjoy their jobs. But mine just changed, it just changed, and there is nothing like running group therapy and having a really good group where things come out. Nothing that I do now can be as stimulating as that.

I have learnt also that the 12 steps is not the only thing. I really did believe for a time it was the only way anyone was going to get well. I have learnt that, at this part of the voyage, it's not. People get well without the 12 steps. They recover emotionally, spiritually, psychologically and can be buoyant, productive, happy and useful people without the 12 steps. I have seen that happen. And that's been a bit of an eye-opener for me. I thought it was all as a result of the 12 steps but that's probably one of the downsides, sometimes we live in a bubble to an extent. Of course you have got to offer people choices, but the 12 steps isn't for everyone. And I know it won't be for everyone. But that mantra gets used by people for the wrong reasons. For example, people who want to maintain their own prescribing position, or because the person is prejudiced and doesn't understand it. I just feel if abstinence is not for everyone it is for bloody most people who have had a serious drug problem because I know a couple of people who have been on heroin and crack for instance and now drink OK. But those two or three people that I know never had an issue with alcohol, they never really drank in their lives so the idea that any chemical is one too many, a thousand isn't enough, hasn't proven to be true so far in these people's lives.

I know for those two or three people, I must know a hundred who have tried to drink when they have been in recovery from heroin and crack or alcohol, people with alcohol who have tried smoking a bit of pot. And they end up messed up. I think there is a lot to be said for abstinence. The jury is probably out, we are all individuals and the jury will probably be out for centuries, I don't know. I don't know if we will ever discover a way to sort this out or why it's happened either. It's frightening. We do well, the outcomes are good but sometimes I also feel like we are brushing leaves up on a very windy day.

Sometimes I despair. Someone has come along for six months, nine months whatever and they leave and you hear within days or weeks that they have gone back out again. And you know that really worries me; when I see the scale of the problem and I don't think people understand addiction. I don't think we are very far along the line, even the likes of you guys who spend your lives researching, and people in AA and NA, and service providers, even people who have been in recovery for a long, long time, I don't think we understand it. It's a huge question. And sometimes I feel like we are just trying to hurriedly make a dam out of matchsticks because the tide is big and it's growing. I think society probably needs to be changed totally and utterly for this to sort itself. The spirit needs to be right and the technicalities will then take care of themselves. But nobody knows how to do that.

(Interview with Rowdy Yates)

Maggie

My name is Maggie and I am an alcoholic – a recovering alcoholic. My last drink was on Friday 13 December 1996. I came to AA for the second time in my drinking career, but this time decided to stay. At this point in time I was at, what most people would say, was an 'all time low' but I could not see this, as I still had my best friend, a half bottle of vodka, in my pocket. I was homeless and unemployable, and although family and friends had done their utmost to prevent my demise, the power that alcohol had over me beat them into the ground as it did me.

Today, nearly 13 years down the line, I have earned the respect of family, work colleagues and friends through living by the guidelines of the AA programme. I do my best today to continue the chain and show to others what was shown to me, by way of kindness and unconditional help and guidance. I have my family back in my life (free from worry), a roof over my head, food to eat and a wonderful husband, all earned in sobriety and these years have been the best years of my life...so far. I owe it all to the continuous support and friendship of my friends and fellow members of AA. I am assured by people older in the fellowship and far wiser than me, that my best day has yet to come. Bring it on.

INT   So what does recovery mean to you?

Maggie   One word that strikes out to me about recovery is freedom: freedom from fear, freedom from people pleasing, freedom of choice; to be able to wake up in the morning without this absolute terror when you are thinking 'what is the matter? What is going on with me?' I don't have that fear any more. I don't have to revolve my day around alcohol; I don't have to worry what other people think of me. I am just totally free to live my life as a 'normal', or so-called 'normal human being', I don't quite know how else to describe it.

I have lived in fear; fear is a big thing with me because I was a very closeted wee child. I have got a picture of myself sitting at the corner of the street because I didn't know how to fit in with anybody because I was frightened and I didn't know what I was frightened of. I didn't know if I was frightened that the others didn't want me; I don't know if I was frightened that they would ask me to do things that I didn't want to do. That kind of fear grows with you and you find yourself going out in the morning walking up to your work and just not knowing why you are scared. Alcohol was the release from that freedom, the alcohol doused out the fear. And that fear has never returned since I have been in recovery and I went straight into recovery on the first day that I came back into the fellowship in 1996.

I went straight into recovery, no time spared, and therefore the fear left me and it's never ever come back to me. It's one of these things that the further on I go the more it gets to me about how great a release this has been. I am not frightened of people; I am free to do things. I am free to get up and dance, and sing, and do things without thinking that the whole world is watching me. I am free not to be perfect, I don't want to be number one in the class any more, I don't want to be put up there with expectations. I am quite happy sitting just being me. I am totally comfortable in my own shoes these days. I have freedom of choice; I am not dictated to by booze, and I am not dictated to by my feelings.

INT   *At what point would you say you were in recovery? Is there a point?*

Maggie   For me I went straight into recovery, plain and simple. I had been around the fellowship prior to 1996. I had come out of hospital after being there for five weeks and I am not rightly sure how long I was around the fellowship because I seemed to be on a different planet. I wasn't taking any substances but my head was on a different plane and although I was around AA I wasn't applying myself, I wasn't on a programme, I wasn't looking at myself and I was very fortunate that when I entered AA as a default (I didn't go to get sober, I went to an AA meeting because I was standing in the streets with nowhere to go, with no money, no roof over my head, thinking I was great, thinking I was fine because I was away from anybody that was going to tell me not to drink). And yet I went and knocked on the door of somebody that I had known in the fellowship and this person knew me of old and knew that if I did not get into recovery from the word go, that I would not stand a chance.

I truly believe for me that if I hadn't gone into the fellowship that day I would be dead or I would have a wet brain. Physically I could have taken drink but mentally I was off my head and this lady actually knew me and knew that she had to get me into recovery straightaway. At my first meeting of AA, which I went to for all the wrong reasons, with no intentions of getting sober, I had what I can only describe as a spiritual experience. I totally felt that somebody had put their arms around me and told me I was going to be all right. And from there I decided to stay, and the lady put a roof over my head and I ate, breathed, and slept the programme for the two or three months that I stayed with her. To such an extent that I made some big decisions, three or four months sober, and I made them as sober decisions and not emotional decisions.

When it came time for me to go back out to work I knew not to go back into the teaching line or try to retrace my steps. I knew what I was capable of doing, and what I was not capable of doing, and I made some very brave decisions about major areas of my life but I knew at the time that these were not fear-based decisions. I had made fear-based decisions all my days, whether it was to get engaged (which I did three or four times), or career moves, or geographical moves or anything else, I had made fear-based decisions all my life. And three or four months into recovery I was making rational decisions which were not fear-based. Not all my decisions were rational and not all my thinking or actions were rational over the next two years, but there was progress in recovery, and an excitement in getting well. For the first time in my life I had no fear of the unknown and I had no expectations of myself other than I wanted to get well. And I feel that recovery kicked in during these months and whenever I think about it, it just underlines it – that's what happened and I love it. I just love it. I really do.

INT   *And now that you have been in recovery for quite a long time what is it you feel that keeps you going in your recovery?*

Maggie   I have been taught that this is an ongoing illness; that any addiction, of a substance or other thing, is a symptom. Alcohol was my drug of choice, and the symptom led me to recovery. But I was also told, and I fully believe this because I can see it in my own actions if I let myself slip back, that my illness is ongoing and grows on a daily basis as I grow older. And therefore my recovery has got to grow at the same rate. The way that somebody described it to me very beautifully is that it's like going up an escalator that is moving downwards – if you don't keep climbing and walking up that escalator, if you just stop and think things are all right, you are going to end up back at the bottom again. And as I go on, I actually need this fellowship more, I need my recovery more, I am enjoying it more, I am learning more about myself. It's a complete unfolding; I call it my onion layers. Once you think you have got one layer off there is another layer lurking underneath, and another one underneath, and more underneath that; I am a work in progress. And until they put me in my box I will continue to be a work in progress. I am also a firm believer that you have got to take action and so my recovery has to be based on action; continuing to work on myself, or working with other people. It's ongoing, but it gets better and it keeps going.

INT   *You mentioned a number of things that help you in your recovery; is there anything that you would specifically draw out?*

Maggie   The people in AA and the AA programme. I needed the support and sometimes tough love. When I had been around the fellowship initially, people were very kind, but kindness doesn't work with somebody like me because I was a lying, thieving, cheating con person when I came in the doors. I was like that all my days. I was a manipulative little girl, and I lied, and I stole and I thieved. What was going to make me any different? The people I met were the same as me; they knew when I was telling lies and when I was not. They saved my life and my payback is to move on and keep the chain reaction going.

    Also I feel that when family and friends finally did come into my life I was surprised that very few people condemned me. Which again helped me to face who I was – but I always had support. I have had support every step of the way. I also feel I have been very fortunate that I have the ability to talk. I know a lot of people find it difficult to pick up a phone and find it difficult to express how they feel. I am not one of these people. I also have a very firm belief that I am not running the show. I can remember vividly what led me into the fellowship and I remember vividly that it had nothing to do with any predisposition on my part, it really didn't. But I would say AA and the support of the people, a few people in particular, and hard work is what has made it for me.

INT   *Is there anything you would say had hindered you or held you back?*

Maggie No. If anything was to hold me back it would be myself. Any times where I have stepped back from meetings, or when I have started to criticize others, then my recovery has taken a backward step. But I cannot accuse anybody of hindering my recovery; I need to take a look at myself because the only person that can hinder my recovery is me. I know what to do, I have got a set of tools; I know how to use them, and it doesn't matter what life throws at me I have been given the tools and I have been given support. I know that I will get support whenever, and wherever I need it. My recovery is nothing to do with externals; my recovery is an inside job. And the minute I start apportioning blame it means that I am off beam and I have got to take it right back to myself. So no, nothing else has held me back.

INT   *Did you go to any other services for help before going to AA?*

Maggie Yes I did. I did that mainly to get people off my back. I had counsellors coming in to see me when I landed back on my mother's doorstep. I was like a boomerang and every time I landed back on my mother's doorstep, from wherever I had gone geographically, my return was more and more dreaded. But the problem was that I never told anyone – counsellors, doctors – the truth. I was in hospital for five weeks and I never told anybody the truth. When I was discharged, the counsellor would come to the house and my mother was always there, I was never allowed to speak to the person on a one to one. And it would end up with my mum and the counsellor speaking over me the whole time. I think he helped my mum more than he did me, because my mum was in so much pain that I think she needed to talk more than me. I remember feeling really angry at one point, when he changed his visit from weekly to fortnightly, mainly because he believed my lies. The only reason I wasn't drinking at that point was because my mother was virtually holding me prisoner. When he said that he would come back in a fortnight, I actually had very hurt feelings that he couldn't be bothered coming to see me on a weekly basis. But saying that, I was just playing the game, and I played the game with everybody. I would tell you what you wanted to hear, and go off and do my own thing. I wouldn't have known the truth if it smacked me in the face but as I say, I think the counsellor did more for my mother than for me, I suppose it gave her a vent.

INT   *And what was it about AA that made a difference for you?*
Maggie I had gone to a couple of meetings because the doctor had told me to, but I had gone drunk so I never took anything out of them, but people in AA knew me because of this. So they came to collect me from hospital. I was really pleased because people at the hospital had arranged for me to go into a flat of my own, which meant my mother wouldn't be keeping my money. I had my benefit book back, and I thought that I had won. I only found out years later that the doctors did not want me anywhere near my mother because she was ready to have a nervous breakdown. But I thought it was all about me so when it came to my first experience of AA I had no interest in it.

My second experience of AA – I went because the woman who took me was putting a roof over my head. I said 'right I will play the game' out of sheer big headedness and with no intentions of getting sober; no intentions of stopping drinking. But I thought I would play the game until I could cash my benefit book. I went to a meeting and I truly believe I had a spiritual experience in the room that night. Something happened to me and I don't remember exactly what happened. It was like somebody had taken this big brace or vice off my head because I just felt a sense of calm.

I went home and finished the drink that I had in my bottle and then I woke up the next morning without the desire to drink. It wasn't a conscious thing, in fact it was the most confusing day I have ever spent in my life because I didn't know why I wasn't running away to get drink. I was in total confusion and I went to meetings at night feeling a wee bit peculiar and seeing these notices at the meeting saying 'you are not alone'. I just know that if I hadn't had that spiritual experience and if I hadn't been put through that programme I would be dead or I would be in an institution. I know that, because I don't know if I had it in me to want to get sober.

I do feel that something happened to me that night and that, coupled with intensive work on the programme, changed me. I stood for days ironing and keeping music and noise on around me. I was far from sane, I really was; my head was all over the place, but after a couple of days I turned around and said 'do you mind if I stay here?' I actually decided that I was going to stay in Scotland, get sober, and I quite liked the peculiarity of the whole thing but I really didn't understand what was going on.

INT   *So you feel you have undergone a big change?*

Maggie It's a radical change; I don't know if you would have liked me very much before that.

INT   *And you have talked about being in contact with other people in recovery. Why is that important to you?*

Maggie If you had asked me that a few years ago, I would have said 'Well I drank 24 hours a day, I need recovery 24 hours a day'. My initial contact with people was circumstantial, I wasn't able to work and I felt I needed people around me all the time. We formed bonds and friendships, and it was exciting. When I wasn't working my whole life revolved around AA because my family didn't want to know me at that point. I was so lucky – all I had to do was get well. And it's only as life is going on that you are curtailed in certain ways. The bottom line is that I did as I was told and I would say that I did as I was told for the first few years. Back then, that is why I thought I kept in touch with other people.

Today I keep in touch with people on different levels, I keep in touch with people for myself; when I need to talk, if there is something troubling me and I can't always go to my husband with it. My husband is also in the fellowship. I keep in touch with people in that way and I keep in touch with people socially. I have got an incredible social life. I have found that women can be nice and women can be fun and women don't have to be bitchy, because the women who are in recovery are not on the defensive. And they are not watching out thinking 'what does she want from me', whereas most people in the outside world would think 'what is she after?' And I have found women in AA who are confident in their own recovery. I found it quite peculiar that they were actually honest in their affection and in their wishes, and they wanted to help me. So I keep in touch on a social basis and I also keep in touch with people when I might be able to do something to help. I have a responsibility, especially to newcomers. I have got to give back some of what was given to me because if we stop doing that then there won't be any fellowship. That happens on a number of levels: I email people, and I pop into visit, and sometimes send wee cards and things. I have always been an active member of an AA group and I am currently involved in sponsorship. And it keeps me out of mischief.

INT   *What supports do you think should be in place for people who are working towards recovery?*

Maggie I don't know exactly what particular supports I would put in place for people but unless you are alcoholic yourself, unless you have got this illness, you can't fully appreciate what it means to recover from it. I think people in outside organizations, whether it be doctors, social workers, employers or whatever, do their best. They do their best as they have been taught and as they see it. My sister is an alcohol counsellor, and we don't talk to each other about the illness because she has been taught this is not an illness. And I would like to see more people who have suffered from this illness and are in long-term recovery themselves, have an opportunity to advise or help with the various services which are on offer. I am sure that people are doing their best with the knowledge that they have of the illness; but self-knowledge is the best knowledge you can have of this illness of alcoholism.

Say, for example, with employment, a boss might be doing their very best for somebody but I have trailed bosses and doctors through the mire with my illness, and the medical profession must be sick of us because we just tell lies. But when people are actually in, or going into recovery, they do need help on various levels, for example I had difficulty in finding housing, writing CVs, and I had to rely on other people to show me how to sort these things out. I wish there was more involvement with people actually in recovery but I don't know how that would happen.

INT   *Do you think there should be more opportunity to combine personal experience with professional knowledge?*

Maggie   Yes I think there is a need for a combination of skills. This is similar to the initial involvement in AA of Dr Silkworth, who worked with alcoholics but hadn't experienced the illness himself. He was open-minded enough to work with the people who initially founded this fellowship. If anybody is reading this who is not an alcoholic, I want them to know that AA can work for anybody and I think it is a case of taking what everybody needs from it. There is no such thing as a hopeless case. And people like me can rise from the ashes, and life is an absolutely amazing rollercoaster. I have enjoyed every single minute of it and I am going to enjoy every single minute more. And recovery is not a punishment, recovery is to be embraced and enjoyed, and we are deserving of it, if we have put the work in and that's all I want to say really.

(Interview with Margaret S. Malloch)

Annemarie W.

Annemarie is from the West of Scotland but she spent many years living in London. Her addiction built up over a number of years. She attended both AA/NA and SMART (Self Management And Recovery Training) recovery groups and still does. She now works in the addiction field professionally in Scotland. She is heavily involved with Wired In, the online recovery community.

INT   *What does recovery mean to you?*

AW   Well, I would define recovery as 'no longer in need of professional services'. And for me, it means – the most important thing it means – is healing. I mean a healing from what my addiction took away from me and the reasons why I became addicted in the first place. So for me, part of it is about a healing of my former life. Because that's what it feels like now. It feels like a past life. So that would be my sort of, stock answer. That I no longer require professional help. I mean, help from addiction professionals. Throughout my own recovery, I've tapped into various recovery tools.

INT   *Can you tell me a little bit about what your recovery was like?*

AW   In the beginning it was very, very frightening because I'd always used the drugs as a solution. So the drugs that I'd used had always been not just about getting out of myself but about numbing the pain that I felt completely unable to cope with when I was dry or when I was clean. So in the beginning, letting go of the actual substances was absolutely terrifying because I believed then – and I suppose I still believe – that they were like a sort of pressure-valve. As if I could take just so much of normal life and then I could take them and they'd release the pressure. So I know they were advantageous for a year because they helped to relieve that pressure and they were, for me, a coping mechanism. So it took me a long time to let go of that belief. That if I didn't use them how was I going to cope? Like, when it became too much, when the pain was too much, what was I going to do? And I was very frightened that I would actually fall apart mentally. Definitely, in my first year of recovery, I sometimes thought I was going to end up cuckoo altogether!! I was just really terrified that I would fall apart and they wouldn't be able to put the pieces back again because I'd used all those substances to keep the pieces together. So I remember the first year as being pretty much fear-based. But because I was surrounded by people who had done it and who had been in recovery for long periods of time, there was enough hope to keep me in with my fear without running away from it.

As I started to get the rewards of staying clean, it got better. I remember, about four or five months into my recovery. It was a winter's night in London. It was pishing with rain and the windows were rattling (I stayed in an old Victorian flat). And I'd got my pyjamas on and I'd made hot chocolate and I'd made peanut butter sandwiches and I'd put the fire on. And I was just sitting in front of the fire. And, it was the first time, I think, I'd ever felt peace. And it quickly turned to joy when I recognized that the feeling that I had was a feeling of peace and that I was safe. And having that experience about four months into my recovery, I got hope then that that feeling would grow. So I hung in through the fear and the pain in order to get more of that feeling into my life. And I had a hope from that point because a lot of the folk around me confirmed that they carried that feeling around with them for a lot of the time. So that was something that I certainly wanted to develop but it was through my own experience of it happening. Other people had talked about it happening in their lives and had said it would happen to me but once I'd experienced it for myself I thought, 'Right. OK. I want more of this!' So that gave me the courage to carry on.

INT   *So was this mainly AA – was that where the support was coming from?*

AW   At that time in my recovery, it was mainly other AA members around me. I got in with a group of young people who sort of, took me under their wing. I was 25 and they were all between 20 and 30. There was a group of six or seven of us. One of the guys was five years clean but everyone else had more than that; like six or seven or eight years. So I was kind of the baby of the group. I was terrified that I was going to give up my life as I saw it. They were the same age as me and they had the same interests. Because I still wanted to be young and do young things – go pubbing and clubbing and do all that stuff. And I was able to do all that because I was in with a group of young people who were in recovery. And they'd established and maintained their recovery first so I was really lucky that I was in a group that was solid and safe.

Probably the last year of my using was the point at which I used the most. I was working full-time and I had two part-time jobs. I'd always worked throughout my addiction and I became aware that I was only working to feed my habit. And I got these two part-time jobs. One of them was in a local hotel-pub and the other was in an Irish club at the weekends. And it just meant that I could use while I was working and that I'd get access to drugs a lot easier and that I'd spend less! At least that was my thinking at the time! In actual fact it did work for a while. You know, I was able to drink and use whatever drugs I was using while I was working because that was the culture in the two clubs I worked in. Everybody did that so it wasn't frowned upon or anything. It was seen as natural.

But what happened during that year as well was that spiritually I became less and less. It was like *Groundhog Day*. Life just became so repetitive and I was going round in circles just to get myself straight. And then, maybe about a week before I stopped using, before I went to my first meeting, I just remember feeling totally dead inside and thinking, 'Is this it?' 'Is this what life is?' I felt just so…not just alone but so defeated. Because I had everything externally and I'd managed to keep all that stuff – like a house and a job and nice gear and all that. But inside it just felt pointless. So about a week before my recovery, I remember, basically, I just got on my knees and I hadn't got on my knees since I was a wean! And I was completely sober. Mind, I was probably coming down off something! And I just said, 'If there is a God, fucking help me,' sort of thing. And I think within days, I ended up at my first meeting.

You know, I had no idea that it was the drugs that were causing all the problems at that point. I really never. And I ended up at my first meeting through various sets of coincidences. I certainly didn't think I needed help until I was in my first meeting. Previous to going into my first meeting, I never saw that it was the drugs that were exacerbating the problems I had.

At that time in London there were about four or five SMART recovery groups. The part of London where I got sober, I lived in Wandsworth, so I went to meetings round about Chelsea and Fulham and Wandsworth South West. There was quite a varied set of people. Still is. And there was quite a lot of influence from treatment centres like the Priory. There were quite a few private treatment centres in that area. So there were SMART groups and I attended them, probably about once or twice a month for the first year. My sponsor was also a psychodynamic and cognitive behavioural therapist (CBT) who was 16 years clean at that point. So I had access to her, certainly in the first few months, on almost a daily basis. We'd meet once or twice a week for about an hour to three hours. There was no set goal or time put on it. I certainly spoke to her, probably every day, for the first year, whether it was on the phone or whatever. She had experienced a lot of the stuff that I had experienced in my childhood, particularly the sexual abuse. She'd also had similar drug-taking habits to me. So it was CBT techniques that she taught me and she put me in contact with SMART groups. And there was influences coming from a lot of stuff. I didn't always know what it was at the time, but there was a lot of stuff spoken about at meetings which wasn't just the 12-step programme. There was a lot of stuff used from Motivational Interviewing. I recognize it now from my training but I didn't know what it was then. It wasn't just pure AA that was used.

INT *It sounds like you tried out a lot – was there anything you avoided?*

AW   In the 1980s when the heroin pandemic hit Scotland, a lot of my friends got addicted to heroin and I'd seen them struggle with methadone programmes and that. I knew that wasn't something I wanted to get in a fight with because I'd witnessed them in that fight for 15 or 20 years. The only thing I was determined about was that I did not want to use methadone. And that was based on my experience and watching my friends' experiences. Becoming addicted to that (methadone) and using on top and getting involved in the whole culture of that. I spent a fair bit of time with some of them during that time when they were trying to get clean and at that time I was probably just starting to experiment. That would have been around 1988 or 1989. I lived in the Gorbals in Glasgow for a while and I was using a lot of the so-called recreational drugs; you know, ecstasy and coke and that. And I was smoking a bit of heroin at that time; with my friends and with other people. So I had a bit of first-hand experience watching them trying to get clean on methadone and I knew it didn't work. So that was my main thing – to avoid methadone at all costs. That wasn't down to any sort of education. I didn't know anything about randomized controlled trials or anything like that. That was just down to watching my friends and what was happening in my own community.

INT   *Can you pinpoint things you feel have been really important to your recovery?*

AW   The thing that's been the most helpful to me in my recovery has been having the support of other addicts. That's been the major thing, without a doubt. Having that therapeutic value of one addict helping another, whether that addict is from AA or Narcotics Anonymous (NA) or whatever. It doesn't really matter how they got clean, it's how they've maintained their sobriety. Having that, being able to identify with another addict and how we think and how we react and how we cope with life. Having access to another addict on the days when I'm not coping too well has been the most significant part of my recovery.

What's been the most dangerous thing for my recovery – and I've been tempted to buy into this at times – is the way that services are so willing to take responsibility for me. Not just addiction services, but services in general are so willing for me to hand over responsibility for my life to them! Even when SMART recovery came to Scotland, I went along to a few of the groups locally and it was just drug workers still working in the old style. Almost the antithesis of what SMART is really. People coming into groups and saying, 'Oh, I never went to college and I missed the doctor's appointment and I'm still really chaotic,' and the drug worker turning round and saying, 'Well don't worry about it, I'll phone the college, I'll make you a new appointment with the GP.' And I suppose the point I'm making is that the ultimate responsibility...I mean, I'm responsible for my life. The majority of these services have let SMART be bastardized so it's being used in the opposite way to how it should be used. So I've come across services where it has been tempting to say, 'Right. OK. I'll give you that and you can deal with it and I'll just carry on my merry way.' So I'm really suspicious of anything, any service that's going to allow me to just carry on, to self-sabotage, any self-destructive behaviour, I'll be tempted by. I know. I've been tempted a few times by that. That's one of the reasons why I bought into AA in the first place. Because they made it very clear: 'We're not going to look after you. You're going to do the work. We're not going to do it for you.' I've got into many long debates and confrontations with addiction professionals about that very thing. That AA is about self-responsibility and I suppose in a way, that's hindered my recovery too. Because instead of doing what I'm supposed to, you know, acting with tolerance, I've acted out a lot of the time with self-righteous anger. Tried to get them to see rather than accepting that they're ignorant. But I've always felt that I had a responsibility to educate them about what the fellowship is like. But what I've learned over the years is that they've got a concept, an idea in their head about what it's like and no amount of arguing from someone who's actually experienced it is going to change that.

I'd definitely like to see much more peer support. I think that's crucial, crucial. It's the most crucial aspect of treatment – or whatever you want to call it – that you can offer somebody who's shown up saying they want to change their life. To actually give them access to somebody who's been there and done it and will guide them or show them how they did it. And give them that hope that they can do it as well. That was the most important thing for me. I had access to people who had done it and knew for themselves what I was going through. The trouble is that services have become so individualized that you don't really get the chance to meet other people who have been on that journey, but you end up just as isolated as you were when you were using.

(Interview with Rowdy Yates)

CHAPTER 9

Recovery, a Clinical Reality

Brian Kidd

Introduction

This chapter will describe a clinician's understanding of the recent evolution of 'recovery' in the area of care and treatment for problem substance use in the UK. It will provide a historical context and give examples of how national approaches and local delivery are being influenced, with recovery having the potential to bridge gaps between the apparently opposing philosophies of care: achieving abstinence or harm reduction. Finally it will identify implications for providers and commissioners of services to improve our ability to help substance users deal with their problems.

Why now? A clinician's history of recovery in the UK

Recovery is not a new term in this field. The term has seen regular use in the context of the 12-step Minnesota model for managing issues of substance misuse. It appears in texts on the support and treatment required to help citizens overcome their substance use problems as early as the mid-nineteenth century (Day 1886) and even then embodies the elements many would recognize if recovery is to be realized – the need for empowerment of individuals to overcome their own problem.

Twentieth century – the British System of care

The 'British System' is often described lovingly as an approach to the problem of illicit substance use which was person-centred, avoided the kind of confrontational difficulties seen in the US (where there was a strong abstentionist bias) and allowed doctors who cared to help people with problems caused by substance use. An alternative analysis suggests that at its start, the 'problem' to be addressed was minimal – as there were very few problem users – and the approach of replacement prescribing which was embodied in the British System was 'a system of masterly inactivity in face of a non-existent problem' (Downes 1988).

There is no doubt in my mind of the tidy pragmatism contained in the British System. But there is also the worrying seed of a minimalist approach to dealing with problems, which are more complex than some are prepared to acknowledge, using simply medical approaches. When we explore the descriptions of what was recommended in the Rolleston Committee reports we can clearly see that replacement prescribing is seen as a part of the solution and not the solution in itself. There is an assumption that physicians will also be helping individuals to address associated problems and a sense that improvement (or recovery) is implicit in the approach.

The British System was the accepted approach until the 1960s when a sudden increase in problematic drug use saw a reaction from the UK Government to increase controls over movement of drugs and a move to reduce General Practitioners' (GPs') prescribing – instead making replacement prescribing a more specialist activity (Royal College of Psychiatrists 1987). This was the preferred approach through the 1960s and 1970s until the appearance of blood borne virus problems in injecting drug users heralded a change of direction. Hepatitis B infections raised initial concerns but it was the link with human immunodeficiency virus (HIV) which made real change happen (Scottish Home and Health Department 1986). In the name of 'harm reduction' community teams were developed to address the rapidly increasing challenge (Advisory Council on the Misuse of Drugs (ACMD) 1988); GPs were again encouraged to prescribe opiates to reduce likelihood of illicit use (ACMD 1989) and the first real UK treatment guideline in 1991 made replacement prescribing with methadone a real consideration for all doctors if dealing with injecting drug users (Department of Health, Scottish Home and Health Department, Welsh Office 1991).

The next 15 years saw a sea-change in delivery. Harm reduction became the norm. In fact it also developed, affecting more social areas of life as professionals moved away from concerns about rehabilitating substance users – acknowledging the degree of challenge this would involve – and developing an approach which aimed to reduce injecting, associated biological, psychological and social risks and death. Prescribing of replacement opiates became a solution for drug-related criminal activity – with development of alternatives to custody schemes and prescribing in prisons. Concerns about child protection saw moves to give more rapid access to treatments aimed at stabilization rather than abstinence for pregnant mothers or families in difficulties. From the mid-1990s to the millennium investment in services was focused on harm reduction.

But the harm reduction approach which seemed to herald a significant change in the 'debate' around how best to address substance misuse has gradually been seen by some as part of the problem. Training of doctors and professionals in the field has emphasized the medical (prescribing) aspect of care with skills around psychological support and social interventions waning. Critics of harm reduction in general and methadone in particular have portrayed the approach as detrimental to progress with users instead 'parked' on methadone. This has gained some political support, particularly from conservative right wing elements. With very high proportions of drug users in treatment on methadone and availability of non-prescribed alternatives reducing, we have seen a more focused confrontation developing. Two key pieces of work have progressed this debate.

Recovery consensus statements 2008

In 2007 the Betty Ford Institute in the US carried out a process to develop a consensus statement on 'recovery', aiming to give a working definition which people involved in the field at all levels could see as relevant (Betty Ford Consensus Panel 2007). This triggered a similar process in the UK, with the publication of the UK Drug Policy Commission (UKDPC)'s version (UKDPC 2008). Both were produced by diverse groups of stakeholders – including service users – and were aiming to influence the development of new strategies being developed in the UK. In the UK group the following statement was agreed: 'The process of recovery from problematic substance use is characterized by voluntarily sustained control over substance use which maximizes health and wellbeing and participation in the rights roles and responsibilities of society' (UKDPC 2008, p.6).

The statement has been taken into the field for comment by a wide group of stakeholders, including users, professionals and strategists. A consistent view is that this statement does seem to capture the correct tone – allowing many views of addiction to be seen as relevant – and potentially opening the discussion to allow a more diverse range of interventions, with potentially more individual significance, to become available. The Royal College of General Practitioners' own consultation found 74% of practitioners supportive of the statement.

'The new abstentionists' and 'the Great Debate'

In 2007 Mike Ashton published his critique 'The new abstentionists' as a special insert in *Druglink*, the 'house journal' of the organization DrugScope (Ashton 2008). This piece critically analysed the evidence to date on treatment effectiveness and raised concerns that there was a sense of a political shift around the UK – with politicians struggling to hold a firm line in support of harm reduction – instead being beguiled by claims that abstinence-based approaches could turn the tide of increasing numbers of problematic drug users and improve our effectiveness. The article stimulated considerable interest and rekindled the 'either/or' debate. In response, DrugScope organized three 'Great Debates' across the UK to allow those working around these issues to hear opinions from those who held polarized views, and to participate in a facilitated discussion on the topic.

It is questionable whether these events were successful, in that the records of the discussions suggest they simply allowed rather fixed views to be aired in a hostile and polarized environment. A summary document was published which tried to ensure the discussion was articulated in an objective and balanced manner (Roberts 2009). The Great Debate may, however, have ensured that, as governments developed their plans for new approaches, they had an awareness of the potential pitfalls of simply pursuing simplistic views of abstinence or harm reduction.

Evidence-based practice in the UK

Any discussion about recovery in the context of problematic substance use must be considered against considerable recent development in terms of evidence-based practice. The UK has developed clinical guidance for medical and other staff since 1991, when the first 'orange guideline' made it clear that methadone prescribing was appropriate as a harm reduction measure and outlined the best practice for delivery of replacement prescribing and detoxification treatments (Department of Health *et al.* 1991). The document was updated in 1999 (Department of Health *et al.* 1999). That version reflected a much improved evidence base as treatment was evolving rapidly across the world. Requirements that doctors delivered appropriate treatments which reflected their training and experience were emphasized, as were the implications should doctors not fulfil their obligations for the drug-using population. As the evidence base developed further a new guideline appeared in 2007 (Department of Health *et al.* 2007).

2007 orange guidelines

The new treatment guideline was the most comprehensive yet. It was produced by a diverse committee of clinicians (from a range of professions), as well as service users and treatment providers from a range of philosophies. It was supported by the commissioning of National Institute for Health and Clinical Excellence (NICE) Guidelines or Technology Appraisals covering all key interventions (NICE 2007a, 2007b, 2007c, 2007d) as well as referring to any live guidance or evidence bases in other associated areas of work (e.g. pain management or mental health issues). For the first time, it addressed psychosocial interventions and emphasized the need for good clinical governance and quality standards in this area of work.

The evidence base in this field is evolving fast. In 16 years, the UK has seen publication of three national guidance documents, each more comprehensive and rigorous than the last. They emphasize the evidence supporting efficacy of medical treatments and challenge those supporting non-medical interventions to develop equally substantial evidence bases. Any promotion of a change of emphasis from harm reduction must accept the need to protect access to interventions which reduce harm.

National Treatment Agency for Substance Misuse – Models of Care

At the same time – in England – the National Treatment Agency for Substance Misuse (NTA) has been developing high quality guidance for commissioners, services and staff to improve delivery of a more person-centred approach to care. First published in 2002 – but continuously evolving – the 'Models of Care' guidance has the potential to address some of the concerns voiced by service users that all roads lead to methadone, and instead require services fully to assess need and help service users to access the interventions they require (NTA 2006). Advice about improved care planning ensures that staff review a person's progress against their agreed goals and creates an environment in which commissioners are required to ensure a full range of options are available. The NTA also commissions services across England and holds services to tight standards regarding access to services. At the same time, it is developing validated, useful clinical tools which can be used to assess improvement – even in those for whom abstinence is a challenge.

So it is clear that evidence-based practice shows many interventions have potential to improve outcomes. Approaches which address individual needs with tailored programmes of care are most likely to deliver sustained recovery. Such approaches are also less likely to pigeon-hole patients into a 'one size fits all' world of either abstinence or harm reduction.

A case example – Scotland: Development of 'The Road to Recovery'

The Scottish Government published its new strategy to address problematic substance use in 2008 (Scottish Government 2008). As a minority government, the Scottish National Party (SNP) administration successfully took their strategy through the Scottish Parliament – it was accepted unanimously – suggesting the pragmatic approach it contained was acceptable to a range of political opinions. The document used the new language of recovery but clearly rejected the view that this was a move away from support for harm reduction. They quoted the United Nations Office on Drugs and Crime (UNODC):

> Harm reduction has often been made an unnecessarily controversial issue, as if there were a contradiction between treatment and prevention on the one hand and reducing the adverse health

and social consequences of drug use on the other. This is a false dichotomy. They are complementary. (UNODC 2008, p.i)

What was new about the strategy was a practical approach to addressing the apparent lack of availability of treatment, the sense of a reduced range of options (medical, psychological and social) available for users and the concern about people being 'parked' on methadone without any attempt to better engage these people in approaches which could improve their prospects. There was an expectation that service users should be encouraged to engage in their own recovery. Services needed to become more aspirational for their patients. Accepting the need for a more personalized approach, they stated: 'In practice recovery will mean different things at different times to each individual... [It] might mean developing the skills to prevent relapse...rebuilding broken relationships... Milestones may be as simple as gaining weight...or building self-esteem. What is key is that recovery is sustained' (Scottish Government 2008, p.23). The document was based on key Scottish documents which aligned Scottish practice with the national and international evidence base.

Methadone review 2007

This review had been commissioned by the previous (Labour) administration in response to rising concerns around the safety of children if there was prescribing of methadone to drug users. The First Minister had announced a review in response to a drug-related death. The Scottish Advisory Committee on Drug Misuse (SACDM) convened a process involving three elements: a survey of users' views of methadone; a query to all NHS Boards in Scotland regarding numbers in treatment, outcomes achieved and governance of practice; and an expert review group to assess these findings as well as the international evidence and report to ministers. The review was published in 2007 (SACDM Methadone Project Group 2007). It concluded that few National Health Service (NHS) Boards could be clear how many people were in treatment and that even fewer had any real means of demonstrating how effective their programmes were. Service users found methadone helpful but were concerned about a lack of choice in terms of treatment options. The methadone review was delivered to the new SNP administration and its findings were strongly endorsed. However, SACDM then requested further work to put the prescribing of methadone into the context of a person with holistic needs.

Essential Care 2008

The result was the document *Essential Care* (SACDM 2008). This was published in 2008 as the product of a large multi-disciplinary and multi-agency group. Echoing a number of international guidance documents in the substance use field – but also considering learning from other areas such as mental health – the document is aspirational and points towards an improved delivery of care in which the service user is central and substitute prescribing remains the treatment of choice: 'replacement prescribing with methadone remains the main plank of medical treatment for opiate dependency... The challenge with methadone is to optimize delivery of harm reduction whilst ensuring that progress to recovery is encouraged, facilitating a way out of methadone treatment whenever appropriate' (SACDM 2008, p.6).

A continuum of care is essential, with improved processes of service commissioning, effective delivery and an expectation that a full range of specialist services is available in every locality. The role of generic services in addressing the needs of substance users – something not always available – is also emphasized. The Executive Summary of the document notes: 'Substance users have the right to the same quality of care as the rest of us' (SACDM 2008, p.5).

Delivering outcomes

So often, government strategies are published and expectations run high, before faltering as the next political wave pulls the attention of officials towards another initiative.

The publication of *The Road to Recovery* (Scottish Government 2008) heralded the initiation of a major process of reform. A 'Delivery Reform Group' – comprising members of key advisory committees – embarked on a redesign of delivery arrangements, culminating in the publication of *A New Framework for Joint Action on Alcohol and Drugs* (Scottish Government 2009). This document was endorsed by the NHS, the Drugs Minister and Confederation of Scottish Local Authorities (COSLA).

In tandem, Audit Scotland published a critique of the effectiveness of Drug and Alcohol Action Teams (DAATs), highlighting their inconsistencies and recommending improved local commissioning based on needs assessment (echoing the findings of the *Essential Care* document the previous year). A new arrangement requiring DAATs to be transformed into Alcohol and Drug Partnerships (ADPs) was required by October 2009 (Audit Scotland 2009).

Reporting of performance was to be sharpened up – with the NHS becoming subject to new HEAT targets on access to services (NHS Scotland's performance management tool) and local authorities required to report on delivery of local outcomes as part of their new 'Single Outcome Agreements'. The government had also made available a Substance Misuse Outcomes Toolkit to aid local outcome development (SACDM Delivery Reform Group 2009). This would allow performance in the area of substance use to be seen alongside performance in more mainstream areas. New resources continued to increase significantly for the years 2008/9 and 2009/10 to support change. Meanwhile the government reviewed all structures to ensure they were fit for purpose (increasing potential to release funds to improve care) and created a specialist 'support function' to help local ADPs to deliver on their new agenda. Voluntary providers were tasked to deliver a Scottish Recovery Consortium which will improve recovery opportunities for users. An independent Scottish Drug Strategy Delivery Commission will hold the Government to account on its own strategic delivery.

So, in Scotland, we have seen national strategic direction responding clearly to the evidence base and its own experts to capture an aspirational approach to recovery, encompassing both abstinence and harm reduction. Significant moves have been made in government to support a realistic view of recovery; investment has been made but those expected to deliver have had their accountabilities sharpened. The concept of recovery has allowed these changes to develop with strong support from parliament – all delivered by a minority government.

Conclusions: What are the implications for clinicians?

Clinicians in this field care passionately about problem substance users. However, staff can be less aspirational than the users themselves – a group who, like all accessing care, wish to be seen as individuals with options. Harm reduction is always a clinical goal, but recovery and the processes underpinning effective care planning require staff and services to be continuously re-assessing the options which users have access to. If services are not meeting users' needs then services should be reshaped. Resources should be effectively used and that means services demonstrating improved outcomes. For clinicians, the concept of recovery will help us in our work. We should embrace it.

References

Advisory Council on the Misuse of Drugs (ACMD) (1988) *AIDS and Drug Misuse – Part 1*. London: HMSO.

Advisory Council on the Misuse of Drugs (ACMD) (1989) *AIDS and Drug Misuse – Part 2*. London: HMSO.

Ashton, M. (2008) 'The new abstentionists.' *Druglink* (Special Insert), Dec/Jan 2008.

Audit Scotland (2009) *Drug and Alcohol Services in Scotland*. Edinburgh: Audit Scotland.

Betty Ford Consensus Panel (2007) 'What is recovery? A working definition from the Betty Ford Institute.' *Journal of Substance Abuse Treatment 33*, 221–228.

Day, H.B. (1886) *The Opium Habit with Suggestions as to the Remedy*. New York: Harper and Brothers.

Department of Health, Scottish Home and Health Department, Welsh Office (1991) *Drug Misuse and Dependence: Guidelines on Clinical Management*. London: HMSO.

Department of Health, Scottish Office Department of Health, Welsh Office, Department of Health and Social Services, Northern Ireland (1999) *Drug Misuse and Dependence: Guidelines on Clinical Management*. London: HMSO.

Department of Health (England) and the devolved administrations (2007) *Drug Misuse and Dependence: UK Guidelines on Clinical Management*. London: Department of Health (England), the Scottish Government, Welsh Assembly Government and Northern Ireland Executive.

Downes, D. (1988) *Contrasts in Tolerance: Post War Penal Policy in the Netherlands and England and Wales*. Oxford: Clarendon Press.

National Treatment Agency for Substance Misuse (NTA) (2006) *Models of Care for Treatment of Adult Drug Misusers: Update 2006*. London: National Treatment Agency for Substance Misuse.

NICE (2007a) *Methadone and Buprenorphine for the Management of Opioid Dependence*. NICE technology appraisal 114. London: National Institute for Health and Clinical Excellence.

NICE (2007b) *Naltrexone for the Management of Opioid Dependence*. NICE technology appraisal 115. London: National Institute for Health and Clinical Excellence.

NICE (2007c) *Drug Misuse: Psychosocial Interventions*. NICE clinical guideline 51. London: National Institute for Health and Clinical Excellence.

NICE (2007d) *Drug Misuse: Opioid Detoxification*. NICE clinical guideline 52. London: National Institute for Health and Clinical Excellence.

Roberts, M. (2009) *Drug Treatment at the Crossroads. What It's for, Where It's at and How to Make It Even Better*. London: DrugScope.

Royal College of Psychiatrists (1987) *Drug Scenes*. London: Gaskell.

SACDM (2008) *Essential Care: A Report on the Approach Required to Maximise Opportunity for Recovery from Problem Substance Use in Scotland*. Edinburgh: Scottish Government.

SACDM Delivery Reform Group (2009) *Delivering Better Outcomes. An Outcomes Toolkit*. Edinburgh: Scottish Government.

SACDM Methadone Project Group (2007) *Reducing Harm and Promoting Recovery: A Report on Methadone Treatment for Substance Misuse in Scotland*. Edinburgh: Scottish Government.

Scottish Government (2008) *The Road to Recovery: A New Approach to Tackling Scotland's Drug Problem*. Edinburgh: Scottish Government.

Scottish Government (2009) *A New Framework for Joint Action on Alcohol and Drugs*. Edinburgh: Scottish Government/COSLA.

Scottish Home and Health Department (1986) *HIV Infection in Scotland: Report of the Scottish Committee on HIV Infection and Intravenous Drug Use.* Edinburgh: Scottish Office.

UK Drug Policy Commission (UKDPC) (2008) *The UK Drug Policy Commission Recovery Consensus Group: A Vision of Recovery.* London: UKDPC.

United Nations Office on Drugs and Crime (UNODC) (2008) *Reducing the Adverse Health and Social Consequences of Drug Abuse: A Comprehensive Approach.* Vienna: UNODC.

CHAPTER 10

Evidence and Policy: Crime and Public Health in UK Drug Policy

Alex Stevens

Introduction

This chapter will consider recent developments in UK drug policy, and especially the role of criminalization in these developments. It starts by looking at the historical background of British drug policy and a theoretical background for its analysis. It moves on to discuss examples of the selective use of evidence to support criminalizing approaches in drug policy. If we look at the historical development of British drug policy, we can view it as an ongoing argument between issues of crime and issues of public health.

British drug policy: An argument between crime and health

- Rolleston committee 1926:
  - care won over criminalization
  - produced the 'British system' of 'benevolent neglect'
  - but doctors still accountable to the Home Office.
- Response to increased drug use in 1960s:
  - tighter controls on doctors

- o   regulation of drug treatment
- o   misuse of Drugs Act 1971.
- Response to 'heroin epidemic' of the 1980s:
  - o   tougher penalties for drug dealers
  - o   Central Funding Initiative – £18 million
  - o   drug strategy 1985 focuses on enforcement and prevention.
- Response to HIV epidemic of the late 1980s:
  - o   relatively quick implementation of harm reduction which was supposed to include abstinence as a goal.

The Rolleston Committee in 1926 was seen as instituting what became known as the 'British System' of prescribing to heroin addicts (Berridge 1999) but this was the subject of much debate. Some doctors were primarily treating people who had become addicted to heroin through prescribed medication by other doctors. They argued that prescribing opiates was necessary for the care of ill people. But there were other doctors, especially prison doctors whose patients were convicted criminals, who appeared before the Committee and argued that addiction was not an issue of care, but was instead an issue of crime. So even before that Committee, which was seen as the birthplace of the medicalization of addiction in this country, there was a debate about whether addiction was an issue of crime or public health.

After the Rolleston Committee, doctors who were prescribing were still accountable to the Home Office rather than the Department of Health for their practices in prescribing heroin. Later on, after these decades of what has been described as 'benevolent neglect', and due to an increase in drug use in the 1960s, the main response, following two Brain Commissions, was to increase controls on doctors, to regulate drug treatment through drug dependency units and also to bring together all the various laws and penal responses to drug use in the Misuse of Drugs Act 1971, which is still in place today.

A further development in the 1980s was the perceived 'epidemic' of heroin use, especially among unemployed young men in the most deprived parts of this country (Pearson 1987). The immediate response of the Thatcher Government was to institute tougher penalties for drug dealers and traffickers through the Control of Drugs Act of 1985 and the Drug Trafficking Offences Act of 1986.

A central funding initiative of £18 million was allocated to drug treatment, which seems a very paltry sum compared to the sums which we see being invested now, but which was seen as a huge sum at the time. The Drugs Strategy implemented in 1985, 'Tackling Drugs Misuse', focused three of its five priorities on enforcement and prevention. There was a very clear emphasis in that drug strategy on using the criminal justice system as the response to drug use.

In the 1980s there was a human immunodeficiency virus (HIV) epidemic and compared to other countries there was a relatively quick implementation of harm reduction, partly based on the works of the Advisory Council on Misuse of Drugs in 1988 but, as Yates (2002) has said, abstinence was seen very much as an ultimate goal. Harm reduction could be employed before individuals achieve abstinence, in order to reduce the rates of HIV, but that that should not preclude moves towards abstinence. This idea recurs.

A theory of policy formation
The 'discourse coalition' approach (Hajer)

- Discourse: A set of ideas and symbols that share common concepts.

- Coalition: A loosely formed group of individuals and organizations who form around a discourse.

- Discourse structuration: The attempt to make a discourse the dominant way of thinking about an issue.

- Discourse institutionalization: The translation of a discourse into laws, practices and policies which express it.

This debate has been going on in British drug policy for a long time now, oscillating between crime and public health as the predominant emphasis. This seems to fit with a theory of policy formation that has been developed by Martin Hajer (1989, 1993). He uses the concept of discourse, which signifies a set of ideas and symbols that share common concepts. So drugs as a crime problem and as a public health problem can each be seen as one of these common concepts, which are shared within a discourse.

Hajer used the idea of a coalition, a loosely formed group of people who form *around* a particular discourse. So, for example, in British drugs policies there is a health discourse, which would bring together doctors, some drug users, drug treatment agencies, maybe some carers of drug users, who believe that health is the primary problem. There is also a crime discourse coalition, which includes the police, most parts of the media and certainly most politicians when they come to comment on drug problems.

These coalitions struggle for what Hajer called 'structuration' of their discourse. 'Structuration' occurs when a particular discourse becomes the dominant way of looking at a particular problem. When a discourse reaches structuration it affects what information will be considered to be reliable about a social problem. As Mary Douglas (1966) described, information is filtered by the extent to which it originates from sources that are seen as reliable and should fit with ideas that are already dominant. Ideas that come from disreputable sources, or that clash too openly with ideas that are already held and accepted, are less likely to access the world of policy making.

Once an idea has reached structuration it is then institutionalized into laws, policies, and practices, which are based on those common concepts that are held in the discourse. These concepts of discourse coalitions, structuration and institutionalization can be used to think about the way that drug policy has been made in this country.

Evidence in British drug policy

- The available evidence on:
  - drug use
  - drug-related health problems
  - drug-related crime.
- Uses of evidence:

- o the Drugs Act 2005
- o cannabis classification
- o the new harm reduction.
- • An excluded discourse?
  - o drug use as non-deviant.

This chapter will present some of the available evidence that I looked at primarily while writing the report for the UK Drug Policy Commission (Reuter and Stevens 2007). I am going to look at three particular uses of evidence in drug policy. The first relates to the Drugs Act of 2005, the second to the recent, rather strange, debate about cannabis classification and the third, to new methods of harm reduction. Finally, I want to look at a discourse that has been excluded from drug policy and that is the idea that drug use can be seen as a non-deviant activity.

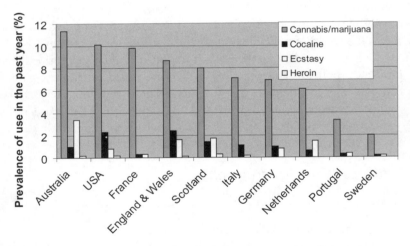

Figure 10.1 Prevalence of past year drug use as measured by population surveys

The evidence in this field, on any of the indicators used here is open for methodological challenges, but is based on the most reliable sources available (Figure 10.1). Data from the various population surveys that have been collected in Europe, America and Australia show that there is no correlation between the amount of penal repression of drug use and the level of drug use in a country. So, for example, Antonio Maria Costa, the executive director of the United Nations Office on Drugs and Crime, has argued that countries 'get the drug problems they deserve' (Costa 2007). He has argued that the Netherlands are too liberal and therefore have got a huge drug problem.

But from the available evidence, it would appear that his statement sends a highly coded message that the US deserves a relatively enormous drug problem due to its high levels of inequality and incarceration. However, given the fact that his office is largely funded by the US, it is unlikely that that is the message he is trying to give. It is more likely that he has misinterpreted the evidence on levels of drug use across countries and the lack of correlation between prohibition, the enforcement of drug laws and rates of drug use.

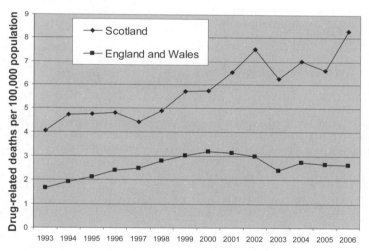

Figure 10.2 Drug-related deaths in the UK

In terms of drug-related harms, death is one of the most important measures and differing trends occur in Scotland, and England and Wales (Figure 10.2). Drug-related deaths have been rising in all three countries up to 2000, when the number seems to have stabilized and even dropped off slightly in England and Wales, while there has been a trend of increasing death in Scotland with 421 recorded deaths in 2006, and 1366 in England and Wales.

By international comparison, the UK has quite high rates compared to Europe (Figure 10.3). Denmark uses a different definition to most of the other European countries, so it may be indeed that the UK has the highest level of drug-related death in Europe. The US has even higher rates of drug-related death than Denmark.

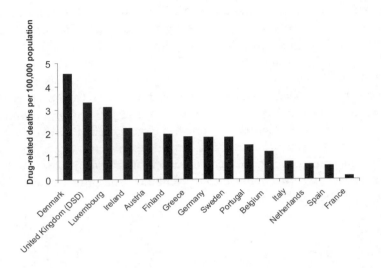

Figure 10.3 Drug-related deaths in Europe

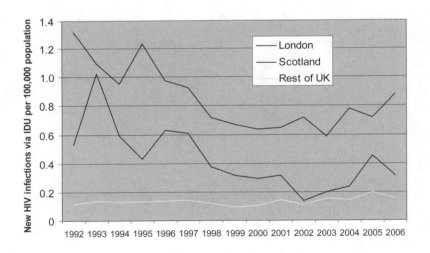

Figure 10.4 New HIV infections via intravenous drug use (IDU)

HIV is another primary health-related consequence of practices associated with injecting drug use. Over the long term it is possible to see a decline of the number of new notifications of HIV associated with injecting drug use. But recently, there seems to be a rather concerning increase in notifications, in both London and Scotland (Figure 10.4).

Comparing national patterns across Europe, Spain has one of the highest levels of HIV amongst injecting drug users, but this has fallen since the early to mid-1990s (Figure 10.5). Before then Spain had a very

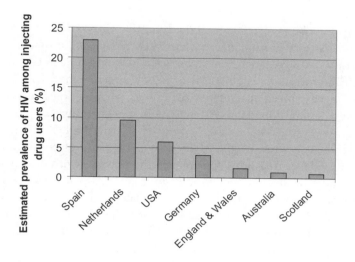

Figure 10.5 Prevalence of HIV among injecting drug users

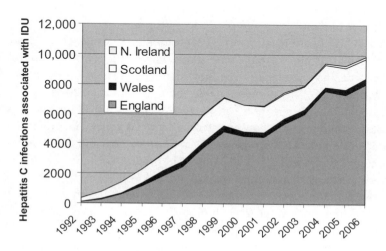

Figure 10.6 Hepatitis C infections associated with IDU

abstinence-focused policy and did not countenance using any harm reduction measures. They have since introduced extensive harm reduction programmes, expanding methadone maintenance treatment and needle exchange (including in prisons) and rates have fallen as a result. But they were so late in implementing these measures that they have been unable to reduce rates of infection to those of the UK.

Hepatitis C is a major concern when it comes to injecting drug use and we see a huge increase in all the countries of the UK. Forty-one per cent of injectors in England and Northern Ireland are estimated to be hepatitis C positive, compared to between 44% and 62% in Glasgow.

Health inequality is obviously a major concern in the UK. Although drug use has spread throughout society, its harmful consequences are felt most severely in deprived communities. According to the British Crime Survey the use of class A drugs is actually higher amongst the most affluent groups, primarily because of high use of cocaine. There is some evidence that drug dependence and related health problems are concentrated in deprived areas and groups. I did some analysis of the survey of psychiatric morbidity from the late 1990s in a multi-variant controlled analysis. It turned out that unemployed people were nearly four times more likely to report drug dependence indicators than those in employment. It is possible to argue about the causal mechanism here. It could be that people who are drug dependent are more likely to lose their job and become unemployed, but it is also likely that people who are unemployed to start with become drug dependent. The causal mechanism might work both ways to reinforce that link between one indicator of deprivation and dependent drug use.

It is also possible to identify a concentration of drug-related death in deprived areas. For example, one study showed that two-fifths of drug-related deaths happened in the most deprived areas in Scotland, where only one-fifth of the population was living (Zador et al. 2005).

Criminal victimization can also be seen as contributing to health problems and it is also concentrated in deprived areas. Tim Hope (2001) studied the links between British Crime Survey data and the UK census. He found that over half of all household property crime is found in the poorest fifth of communities in England and Wales.

So, in summary, the evidence on drugs and health indicates that drug-related death is relatively high by international levels and rising in Scotland. Rates of HIV are quite low by international levels. The UK has experienced high rates of hepatitis C which have been rising consistently over the last few years, and drug dependence would appear to contribute to health inequality.

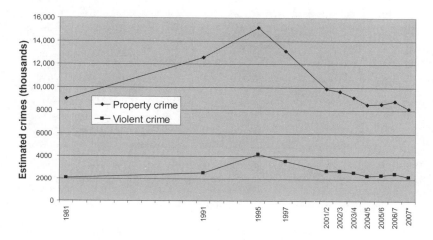

Figure 10.7 Crime estimated by British Crime Survey, 1981–2007

In relation to the evidence on crime, there appears to be a peak in levels of recorded crime in 1995 and a significant reduction since then (Figure 10.7). Certainly, in relation to property crime there has been quite a significant reduction in the most common types of crime. Drug use is considered as a crime and there are drug-related offences that can lead to imprisonment. In England and Wales penal responses to drug offenders have become increasingly harsh, if we take the use of imprisonment as an indicator of harshness. In Figure 10.8 we see a 150% increase in the number of years that have been given by courts in England and Wales for drug-related offences since 1994.

Estimates of the proportion of crime that is caused by drug use shift depending on which politicians are using them and what definitions are used. I did an analysis of the policy discourse around the creation of the Drug Treatment and Testing Order in England and Wales. In parliamentary speeches, the lowest estimate of drug-related crime was 20%, related to burglary by Joy Mott in the late 1980s (Mott 1986) and the highest was given by Tessa Jowell (Jowell 1997) who argued that 70% of crime was committed by drug users, based on an anecdotal report from the Chief Constable of the West Midlands. But in between this range, people seem to have settled on the figure of around 50%. For example, a consultation document for the new Welsh drugs strategy

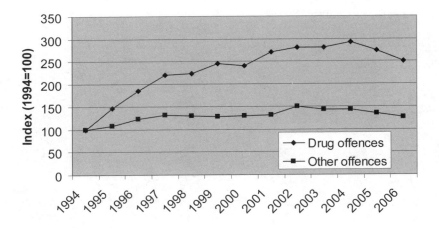

Figure 10.8 Trend in number of years of imprisonment handed out by courts, England and Wales, 1994–2006

(Welsh Assembly Government 2008) claims: 'It has been estimated that drug motivated crime accounts for half of all crime.'

The estimated cost of drug-related crime is approximately £13.9 billion per year (Godfrey, Stewart and Gossop 2004). Now, the problem is that these estimates on the *proportion* of crime and the *value* of crime related to drugs have been exaggerated by taking their basis in studies of arrestees and drug users in treatment. By focusing only on those drug users whose drug use has become so problematic that they have to go to treatment or have ended up in the police station, you are looking at a specific and relatively small proportion of the drug user population. For example, discussion of the proportion of crime that has been related to drugs normally refers to surveys of arrestees, such as the new English and Welsh Arrestee Drug Abuse Monitoring (ADAM) study. People have extrapolated from that study to try and work out what proportion of crime is caused by drug users.

Using the British Crime Survey it is possible to estimate that only about 6 of every 100 offences leads to the identification of the offender. The new ADAM study estimates that 31% of people use class A drugs, and 69% of people have used any drugs prior to being arrested. This applies only to the small proportion of arrestees who were included in the ADAM study. We have no idea if it applies to the larger figure of offenders who have not been arrested.

Criminological research has highlighted the various ways in which the police discriminate when they choose who to arrest, and that might not be because they are deliberately discriminating against certain groups. It might just be easier for them to go to a group of people who they suspect are more likely to provide good results for them, and so it may be that they are more likely to go and arrest drug users.

I tried to test this hypothesis by looking at data from the Offending, Crime and Justice Survey, which is a self-report household survey of 10–25-year-olds. And amongst those 10,000 people that they interviewed, 1370 of them said that they had been offending in that year. Out of those people, I looked at how many said they had been arrested in that year. Table 10.1 shows the odds ratios for those variables which predict whether a person said they had been arrested. Criminologically you would expect factors such as being male and of ethnic minority (specifically black, or mixed ethnic minority origin) to predict whether the police would arrest an individual in any given year. It is interesting that those people who are employed or in education were much less likely to be arrested after they committed an offence than those people who are unemployed. Individuals who had used drugs in the previous year were about twice as likely to be arrested as those who had not used drugs. Most revealing is the finding that the frequency of offending, defined by prolific offending (considered in the survey as six offences or more), was not a significant predictor of whether an individual was arrested or not, whereas drug use was.

Table 10.1 Logistic regression of data from *Offending, Crime and Justice Survey* **showing predictors of reported arrest among self-reported offenders, aged 10–25 (n=1370)**

	Odds ratio	Significance (p)
Sex is male	2.15	<0.05
Older age	1.11	n/s (not significant)
Ethnicity is black or mixed	2.71	<0.05
Prolific offending	0.91	n/s
Ever truanted	1.68	n/s
Ever excluded from school	0.94	n/s
In work or education	0.32	<0.01
Any drug use in previous year	1.91	<0.05

This has been backed up by the Edinburgh Study on new transitions into crime, in which McVie and MacAra have done a very similar analysis of their data and shown that drug use is a predictor of whether an individual gets in trouble with the police (McAra and McVie 2005). The mechanisms that may underlie this are illustrated by Rhodes *et al.* (2007) who did a qualitative study with drug injectors in South Wales. The respondents spoke about 'constant supervision by the police'. This is what Reiner (Reiner 2000) calls 'statistical discrimination'. When the police have limited resources, they may be more likely to try and maximize their results by arresting particular groups of people. This can result in the constant supervision of drug users, therefore boosting the rate at which drug users are arrested and leading to exaggeration of the proportion of crime that is attributed to drug users when these arrestees are surveyed in studies like ADAM.

The estimated £13.9 billion cost that allegedly results from drug-related crime comes from the National Treatment Outcome and Research Study (NTORS). It is calculated by asking the 1075 users who entered the study about offending in the previous three months, and then extrapolating from that to the estimated 327,466 drug users in the country. The problem with the figure is that it assumes that people report their offending accurately, and then extrapolates this from the three months to the whole year. It also makes a huge assumption that people who come into treatment are offending at the same rate as all those 327,466 problematic drug users. That is not a safe assumption, because it is well known in treatment research that offending tends to peak in the months and years before treatment entry. So what is happening is that NTORS are extrapolating this peak figure to the whole population for all the time that people use these drugs. The £13.9 billion figure is therefore an exaggeration of the cost of drug-related crime.

To summarize on drugs and crime: crime is falling; the proportion of crime committed by drug users is likely to be less than has been estimated and used in policy debates; and the cost of crime by drug users is also likely to be less than has been estimated. There is also some doubt about the causal relationship between drugs and crime and the search is on for a third variable that might explain this relationship, rather than just simply assuming that drug use causes crime.

So let's move on to examples of how this available evidence has been used in policy. The first example I am going to use is the Drugs Act of 2005. This can be seen, as one MP put it, as a piece of pre-election window dressing. It came up in the months before the 2005 general election and was rushed through parliament before that election. But it can also be seen as an attempt to use some of the evidence on drug problems based on the work of John Birt. He is the former Director General of the BBC who was brought in by Tony Blair to be his 'blue sky thinker' in the Cabinet Office. Under John Birt's leadership, the Prime Minister's Strategy Unit in the Cabinet Office produced a report about drug problems which, it can be argued, led to some of the measures in the Drugs Act 2005.

This report from the Prime Minister's Strategy Unit (PMSU) was written in the form of 105 PowerPoint slides. There were 12 slides on crime and 2 on health, showing the relative importance of crime against health problems as viewed by Birt. The utilitarian calculation of crime seems to have been deemed more important than health, based again on the exaggerated figure of the value of drug-related crime. This is an example of the structuration of the crime discourse; the idea that crime becomes the dominant filter through which we look at drug problems.

And the policy suggestion they came up with in response to this was – to use John Birt's favoured phrase – to 'grip high harm causing users' (all people using heroin and crack considered 'high harm causing users' by definition). Other suggestions were to move the funding and accountability for drug treatment from the Department of Health to the Home Office, make heroin use an offence and, importantly, introduce compulsory testing on arrest.

Compulsory testing on arrest was included in the Drugs Act 2005, which also created the intervention support order to run alongside antisocial behaviour orders (ASBOs), as well as a whole new list of crimes, or aggravating circumstances to existing crimes. These included: classification of magic mushrooms in class A; a presumption of supply for people caught with certain, undefined amounts of illicit drugs (which has been very difficult to implement) and dealing near schools.

Interestingly, in terms of the translation of what was in the PMSU report to the Drugs Act in 2005, new offences included that of refusing a drug test at arrest and refusing to be assessed for treatment, thereby enabling this 'gripping of high harm causing users' that the Prime Minister's Strategy Unit had asked for.

According to one of the civil servants who was involved in the process, the team working for John Birt was interested in the idea of heroin-assisted treatment and its potential for crime reduction. But he said, 'the evidence we found was not what the ministers wanted to hear'. Again this is an example of selective filtering according to a dominant perception of the drug problem being about crime and not about treatment.

A second example is the UK cannabis kerfuffle. In effect, especially in Scotland, it has made no difference whatsoever to anything that anybody does on the street or in their student bedrooms. It appears to be a Westminster-created and Westminster-discussed kerfuffle.

The downgrading of cannabis to class C in 2004 and its reclassification to class B in 2009 has been much discussed. It is worth noting that cannabis use apparently continued to fall throughout this period in England and Wales, but continued to rise in Scotland. Scotland actually implemented the re-classification downwards less extensively than England. The English police stopped arresting people for cannabis use, while the Scottish police did not. This suggests, at least, that there is little correlation between the policing of cannabis and rates of its use.

If we look at the evidence on cannabis, there is no risk of fatal overdose. The Prime Minister has claimed on various breakfast TV sofas that skunk is 'lethal', but this claim does not have any basis in the evidence. There does seem to be a significant association with schizophrenia, but there is an ongoing debate about causality in this link. There is some evidence of association with cancer and heart disease, which would be expected from the idea that smoking carcinogens tends to be bad for the lungs.

There is no evidence that legal changes affect patterns of use. This can be seen from the Scottish and English experience, but also from the 11 US states that have decriminalized the possession of cannabis, in the Dutch experience and in the Western Australian states that have introduced de facto decriminalization of cannabis. There has been no evidence of increased use of cannabis in those areas.

Politicians' statements on reclassification back to class B assumed that we can use the criminal law in a telegraphic way; that the law is the appropriate means for sending messages to young people about young people. And accordingly the experts at the ACMD have been ignored and measures put in place to further criminalize cannabis users. Here again we have evidence of selective filtering. A debate about health has been translated into a policy response that criminalizes young people. And so again the idea that drugs are a criminal matter has been institutionalized and then structured by the legal response to the use of cannabis.

The third example is about new methods that have been proposed to implement harm reduction. There is evidence of increases in death, HIV and hepatitis C and also risky injecting among injecting drug users.

This suggests that we need to reinforce efforts to reduce risky injecting, to reduce fatal overdoses and the spread of blood borne viruses. And this seems to be especially true for vulnerable groups, such as young people who are starting to inject or are at risk of becoming injecters; heroin users who have not engaged with, or who have dropped out of, existing forms of treatment, and prisoners.

Some of the methods proposed include: outreach peer and care interventions; training drug users and carers of injecting drug users in the use of emergency naloxone in order to reduce deaths from overdose. One particularly interesting approach is the use of drug consumption rooms. These are places for the hygienic consumption of drugs that people have already obtained, with trained staff available to engage with those drug users and help them if they experience any problems when they inject. Drug consumption rooms are available in Germany, Switzerland, the Netherlands, Spain, Norway, Luxembourg and Canada and they have been extensively evaluated with the results so far suggesting that they are effective in reaching homeless drug users, who are especially at risk of public injecting, considered to be a much more risky way of injecting. The evaluations tend also to find reductions in risk behaviour and in public nuisance, littering and the careless disposal of injecting equipment (Hunt and Lloyd 2008).

Another interesting approach is heroin-assisted treatment, which has now been evaluated in Switzerland, Germany, the Netherlands and Spain (and an evaluation is also under way in England). Heroin-assisted treatment is not just about prescribing heroin. It provides heroin for on-site injecting along with psychosocial support to people who have not been able to stabilize their use in methadone treatment and so are considered to be a particularly hard group to work with. The results from the evaluations have been that heroin-assisted treatment reduces the use of illicit heroin; the people who receive this treatment tend to improve their health; they reduce the amount of offending they are involved in and also they tend to increase their rates of employment (Uchtenhagen 2008). And in Switzerland there is some indication that rates of initiation into heroin use have reduced, as heroin use has been medicalized and so appears boring to people entering drug scenes (Nordt and Stohler 2006).

A final example is prison needle exchange, which was first introduced in Switzerland and has since spread to Germany and Spain and is just about to be introduced in Portugal. There is currently debate in Scotland about prison needle exchange. Several evaluations have been carried out internationally on prison needle exchanges. They show that some of the fears that are consistently expressed about prison needle exchange, especially from prison officers, such as the likelihood of being attacked with a needle, have not been realized. The needle exchanges appear to have prevented new cases of HIV or viral hepatitis. They have not led to increased drug use within prisons and there have been no reports of initiations into injecting (Stöver *et al.* 2008).

The political response to the evidence is interesting. Drug consumption rooms and heroin-assisted treatment have received quite a different response from politicians in England. Drug consumption rooms were rejected. The Home Office argued that they lead to localized dealing problems, antisocial behaviour and increases in acquisitive crime. But these claims were based on speculation, with no reference to the evaluations that have actually been done on drug consumption rooms.

Heroin-assisted treatment, on the other hand, has been cautiously accepted, dependent on the results of the pilots that are currently going on. And I would suggest here that we might be able to explain the difference between these initiatives. Heroin-assisted treatment is consistent with the idea that is prevalent within the health discourse that, while it is important to treat drug users, it is also necessary to have them under surveillance, to supervize what they are doing, in order to reduce the problems that they cause. And heroin-assisted treatment is more consistent with that idea than are drug consumption rooms, which are more consistent with the rejected discourse that sees drug use as something that can be normal and freely chosen.

This is the discourse of drug use as non-deviant. It relates to the idea of 'normalization' of drug use; that drug use has become normal because it has been accepted in culture and accommodated by most people (Parker, Aldridge and Measham 1998). This idea has been frequently misinterpreted to mean that either the majority of people *are* using illicit drugs, or that people *should* be taking drugs. That is not what I am arguing. I *am* suggesting that drug use can be non-deviant. The deliberate use of substances to change brain functions is a 'human universal'; all the cultures that have been studied by anthropologists have some use for mind-altering techniques and substances (Brown 1991). Drug use can be, as the new deviancy theorists of the 1960s and 1970s argued, goal-oriented, purposeful and rational (Young 1971).

British drug policy, we have seen, is the result of ongoing arguments between crime and health discourse coalitions. In recent years, evidence has been used selectively to support the criminalization of drug users and also of drug services. There is evidence of the institutionalization of drug use as a crime problem, with treatment agencies and treatment responses being subsumed into that framing of the problem. This is one of the reasons why the criminal justice system has become increasingly seen as a pathway to recovery; that people need to go through the criminal justice system before they can recover. The dissenting idea that drug use can be non-deviant has had very little effect on policy, because it shares no discursive affinity with the idea that drug use is a deviant activity.

References

Berridge, V. (1999) *Opium and the People*, rev. edn. London: Free Association Books.

Brown, D.E. (1991) *Human Universals*. New York: McGraw-Hill.

Costa, A.M. (2007) 'Cannabis…call it anything but "soft".' *The Independent on Sunday*, 25 March. Available at www.independent.co.uk/news/uk/crime/antonio-maria-costa-cannabis-call-it-anything-but-soft-441735.html (accessed 14 December 2009).

Douglas, M. (1966) *Purity and Danger: An Analysis of Concepts of Pollution and Taboo*. London: Routledge and Kegan Paul.

Godfrey, C., Stewart, D. and Gossop, M. (2004) 'Economic analysis of costs and consequences of the treatment of drug misuse: 2-year outcome data from the National Treatment Outcome Research Study (NTORS).' *Addiction* 99, 697–707.

Hajer, M.A. (1989) *City Politics: Hegemonic Projects and Discourse*. Aldershot: Avebury.

Hajer, M.A. (1993) 'Discourse Coalitions and the Institutionalisation of Practice: The Case of Acid Rain in Britain.' In F. Fischer and J. Forester (eds) *The Argumentative Turn in Policy Analysis and Planning*. Durham, NC: Duke University Press.

Hope, T. (2001) 'Crime Victimisation and Inequality in Risk Society.' In R. Matthews and J. Pitts (eds) *Crime, Disorder and Community Safety: A New Agenda?* London: Routledge.

Hunt, N. and Lloyd, C. (2008) 'Drug Consumption Rooms: Between Evidence and Opinion.' In A. Stevens (ed.) *Crossing Frontiers: International Developments in the Treatment of Drug Dependence*. Brighton: Pavilion Publishing.

Jowell, T. (1997) In *Hansard: 19th November 1997. Column 431*. London: Stationery Office.

McAra, L. and McVie, S. (2005) 'The usual suspects? Street-life, young people and the police.' *Criminal Justice* 5, 5–36.

Mott, J. (1986) 'Opioid use and burglary.' *British Journal of Addiction* 81, 671–677.

Nordt, C. and Stohler, R. (2006) 'Incidence of heroin use in Zurich, Switzerland: A treatment case register analysis.' *Lancet* 367, 9525, 1830–1834.

Parker, H., Aldridge, J. and Measham, F. (1998) *Illegal Leisure: The Normalization of Adolescent Recreational Drug Use*. London: Routledge.

Pearson, G. (1987) *The New Heroin Users*. Oxford: Basil Blackwell.

Reiner, R. (2000) *The Politics of the Police*, 3rd edn. Oxford: Oxford University Press.

Reuter, P. and Stevens, A. (2007) *An Analysis of UK Drug Policy*. London: UK Drug Policy Commission.

Rhodes, T., Watts, L., Davies, S., Martin, A., Smith, J., Clark, D., Craine, N. and Lyons, M. (2007) 'Risk, shame and the public injector: A qualitative study of drug injecting in South Wales.' *Social Science & Medicine* 65, 572–585.

Stöver, H., Weilandt, C., Zurhold, H., Hartwig, C. and Thane, K. (2008) *Final Report on Prevention, Treatment, and Harm Reductions Services in Prison, on Reintegration Services on Release from Prison and Methods to Monitor/Analyse Drug Use among Prisoners. SANCO/2006/C4/02*. Bremen: Universität Bremen, WIAD Wissenschaftliches Institut der Ärzte Deutschlands gem. e. V. and ZIS Centre for Interdisciplinary Addiction Research (CIAR).

Uchtenhagen, A. (2008) 'Heroin-Assisted Treatment in Europe: A Safe and Effective Approach.' In A. Stevens (ed.) *Crossing Frontiers: International Developments in the Treatment of Drug Dependence*. Brighton: Pavilion Publishing.

Welsh Assembly Government (2008) *Working Together to Reduce Harm – The Substance Misuse Strategy for Wales 2008–2018*. Cardiff: Welsh Assembly Government.

Yates, R. (2002) 'A brief history of British drug policy, 1950–2001.' *Drugs – Education Prevention and Policy 9*, 113–124.

Young, J. (1971) *The Drugtakers: The Social Meaning of Drug Use*. London: Paladin.

Zador, D., Kidd, B., Hutchinson, S., Taylor, A., Hickman, M., Fahey, T., Rowe, A. and Baldacchino, A. (2005) *National Investigation into Drug Related Deaths in Scotland, 2003*. Edinburgh: Scottish Executive.

CHAPTER 11

Recovery, Desistance and 'Coerced' Drug Treatment

Tim McSweeney

Introduction

Since the mid-1990s Britain has pursued a policy aimed at ensuring that those problem drug users caught up in the criminal process receive not only punishment following charge or conviction, but the opportunity to access appropriate drug treatment and social care to help them address any presenting needs. A key consideration for this policy has been to reduce 'drug-related' crime by tackling the association consistently found between some forms of illicit drug use and particular offences (Bennett, Holloway and Farrington 2008). Commitment to, and investment in, this policy has increased considerably over the last decade, arguably placing Britain ahead of most European countries and well ahead of the US in attempting to strike a more enlightened balance between the punishment and treatment of drug misusing offenders. Consequently, the criminal justice system (CJS) is now a significant source of referrals for drug treatment services: 23% of admissions to structured treatment interventions in England during 2007 and 2008 were the result of referrals from the CJS (compared with 19% in 2001 and 2002) (National Treatment Agency for Substance Misuse (NTA) 2008, p.38).

This is not to say, however, that there have not been a range of philosophical, ethical and practical objections raised about the increasing use of the CJS as a conduit into drug treatment services (Hunt and Stevens 2004; Parker 2004; Stimson 2000), while others continue to express some uncertainty about aspects of the theoretical and conceptual framework underpinning these approaches (Seddon 2006, 2007; Seddon, Ralphs and Williams 2008; Stevens 2007). Moreover, the British evidence base to demonstrate the effectiveness of many of these interventions is either limited or non-existent (Holloway, Bennett and Farrington 2005; UK Drug Policy Commission (UKDPC) 2008). Concerns have consistently been expressed too about the scope for CJS-based interventions to facilitate recovery, desistance and reintegration amongst drug misusing offenders (Buchanan 2004; McSweeney, Turnbull and Hough 2008).

This chapter seeks to:

- offer some definitions of recovery, desistance and 'coerced'[1] treatment

- consider why these issues are important

- assess the extent to which one form of 'coerced' treatment in Britain contributes towards promoting recovery and desistance (relative to 'voluntary' forms) by providing an overview of the use of drug treatment and testing orders (DTTOs) and presenting English evidence of their effectiveness from a recent European study

- identify barriers that inhibit recovery and desistance using this particular approach.

Definitions

There are currently no standard or universally agreed definitions of recovery, desistance or 'coerced' treatment, reflecting in part the contentious and divisive nature of these issues, but also some of the limitations inherent within existing theory and research. In relation to the latter, for example, 'terms such as "involuntary", "incentive-based", "legal referral" and "compulsory" treatment have been employed interchangeably – often without any effort to directly assess the client's

---

1   Inverted commas are used around the term 'coerced' to acknowledge that some people may perceive no pressure when they enter treatment as a consequence of the contact with the CJS or pressure from a variety of other sources.

subjective perception of the referral process' (Farabee, Prendergast and Anglin 1998; McSweeney, Turnbull and Hough 2008, p.22). Stevens and colleagues (2005a) recently described 'quasi-compulsory treatment' as any form of drug treatment that is motivated, ordered or supervized by the criminal justice system but which takes place outside prisons.

In an effort to explore the policy implications to emerge from the criminological desistance literature, Weaver and McNeill have also noted a distinct lack of consensus on some fundamental definitional issues in this particular field of study. They have observed how 'most empirical measures typically identify individuals who evidence a significant lull or crime-free gap in the course of a criminal career' but also point to the importance of research which 'considers the desistance process as a decline in the frequency and severity of offending' as people 'zig-zag' and oscillate between phases of conformity and periods of criminality (2007, p.9). With this in mind they highlight the value of a distinction between primary and secondary desistance, as described by Maruna and Farrall (2004). While primary desistance is concerned with the achievement of a significant lull or cessation in offending, secondary desistance refers to the dynamic processes which facilitate an underlying change in self-identity wherein the ex-offender assumes the role of a 'changed person' and labels him or herself as such (see also Burnett and McNeill 2005). Secondary desistance, Weaver and McNeill argue, may be of great significance for rehabilitative efforts aimed at those with deeply entrenched criminalized and deviant identities.

There is also likely to be considerable utility in distinguishing between primary and secondary forms of recovery from dependent patterns of illicit drug use. In other words the mechanisms which facilitate a significant lull or cessation in problematic patterns of illicit drug use are likely to be qualitatively different from those processes which then sustain longer-term recovery – however this is defined (see Best *et al.* 2008). White has previously argued that:

> designation of the status of recovery (partial or full) should be based on the presence of three criteria:
>
> • sustained cessation or reduction in the frequency, quantity, and (high risk) circumstances of AOD [alcohol and other drug] use following a sustained period of harmful use or dependence…;
>
> • absence of, or a progressive reduction in, the number and intensity of AOD-related problems; and

- evidence of enhanced global (physical, cognitive, emotional, relational, educational/occupational, ontological) health.

(White 2007, p.236)

It is these inclusive definitions of recovery, desistance and 'coerced' treatment which are employed throughout this chapter.

The significance of these issues

Developing a better understanding of the dynamic relationship and interaction between recovery and desistance processes, and the role of 'coerced' forms of treatment in facilitating these, is of great significance for a range of theoretical, ethical and practical reasons. On a theoretical level, for example, it has previously been noted that 'considerable parallels in conceptual constructs and analytical techniques exist in studies of the drug abuse career and the criminal career' (Hser, Longshore and Anglin 2007, p.523). Indeed, as Gossop and colleagues have observed using data from the English National Treatment Outcome Research Study (NTORS), 'the factors associated with giving up drugs could be related to those associated with giving up crime' (2005, p.300). Yet it has also been observed how 'drug use and its lifestyle concomitants bring together a host of distinct social network dynamics that uniquely complicate desistance processes' (Schroeder, Giordano and Cernkovich 2007, p.213).

While there may be both sound reasons and evidence to support the use of drug treatment as a vehicle for initiating recovery and desistance processes (Gossop *et al.* 2003; Prendergast *et al.* 2002), the use of the CJS as a route to treatment continues to present a range of complex ethical issues. Perhaps most notable among these is the increasing shift from coercion (which involves an element of constrained choice) towards outright compulsion (e.g. with recent arrangements in many British areas for testing on arrest), with allied concerns about net-widening, proportionality and effectiveness (Hunt and Stevens 2004; Stevens *et al.* 2005b). The rapid expansion in the range of CJS options targeting drug misusing offenders since 1997 also comes at considerable public expense: over £330 million for adult interventions in England and Wales during 2006 and 2007 (UKDPC 2008).

How might 'coerced' treatment contribute towards recovery and desistance processes?

Although considered within the specific context of effective resettlement, Maguire and Raynor (2006) have also provided a useful conceptual framework for understanding the processes and mechanism by which 'coerced' forms of treatment might facilitate efforts aimed at promoting recovery and desistance. In doing so they state that recovery and desistance are best conceived as complex processes rather than discrete events. In making this point the intention is less about subverting aspirations for recovery as being unrealistic, but rather to stress that the impact of any CJS-based interventions may need to be considered and interpreted more within a 'career' perspective as described by the broader recovery and criminological desistance literature. These perspectives have charted the trajectories of drug use and offending careers – with a beginning (initiation/onset), middle (increased frequency of use/offending and associated problems) and end (recovery/desistance) – over the course of many years, with intermittent contact with drug treatment services and the CJS during this time (Best, Day and Morgan 2006; Farrington *et al.* 2006; Hser *et al.* 2007).

In highlighting the significance of developing both human and social capital, Maguire and Raynor emphasize the importance of ensuring access to timely and appropriate forms of support at 'key turning points' (e.g. following arrest or conviction). These turning points can provide important windows of opportunity to develop motivation, skills and capacity for change. This can involve applying a range of techniques and approaches (e.g. motivational interviewing or prosocial modelling) (Harper and Hardy 2000; McNeill *et al.* 2005) with a view to developing thinking skills, attitudes, narratives and roles and responsibilities. Tackling social problems and issues related to integration are fundamentally important too (i.e. housing, relationships and employability). Doing so provides important opportunities to use new skills and adopt alternative roles or narratives.

However, delivering effective forms of integrated support to drug misusing offenders in this way presents obvious and considerable challenges in practice (Farrall 2002; McSweeney, Turnbull and Hough 2008; UKDPC 2008).

Does 'coerced' treatment contribute towards achieving these goals?

In order to assess the extent to which 'coerced' forms of treatment might contribute towards facilitating efforts aimed at promoting recovery and desistance, the remainder of this paper focuses specifically on the use and effectiveness of drug treatment and testing orders (DTTOs). Introducing these disposals formed a central plank of the New Labour Government's manifesto pledge in the mid-1990s to tackle drug-related crime and they have been a key component of successive national drug strategies since then. A focus on DTTOs also lends itself to a valuable north/south comparison to illustrate some important differences in how operational contexts and approaches to implementation and delivery can impact upon processes and outcomes.

Case study: The DTTO

Introduced by the 1998 Crime and Disorder Act, the main aim of DTTOs as a CJS intervention was to reduce drug-related offending using structured drug treatment to tackle substance misuse and dependency. Influenced by evidence from the US drug court model, the approach sought to build on the promising results from earlier probation-led treatment interventions in Britain (e.g. Hearnden and Harocopos 1999), which pointed towards benefits for some drug-misusing offenders accessing treatment as part of their probation supervision. An important distinction between the DTTO and pre-existing arrangements was the use of drug testing and court reviews in an effort to promote compliance and behaviour change with these new requirements imposed by the courts.

In an effort to increase both the number and range of offenders accessing this type of support (DTTOs originally targeted 'high-tariff' offenders on the cusp of a custodial sentence), provisions contained within the 2003 Criminal Justice Act now enable the courts in England and Wales to impose a community order with a drug rehabilitation requirement (DRR). For all intents and purposes the DRR is equivalent to a DTTO in many respects, but there is more scope for greater flexibility when it comes to the supervision and management of these disposals: attendance requirements now range from one contact to 15 hours of supervision each week depending on needs, risks and seriousness of an offence. (In contrast, the DTTO set a blanket 20-hour a week requirement during the early stages of the order.)

Since their introduction in Britain on a pilot basis during the late 1990s there have been in excess of 60,000 DTTOs imposed by the courts (though there was a much slower and piecemeal implementation process across Scotland between 1999 and 2004). However, courts in England and Wales have had a greater propensity to impose DTTOs than their counterparts north of the border: the incidence per 10,000 of the adult (aged 16 plus) population during 2006 and 2007 was 1.7 in Scotland and 3.6 in England and Wales (McSweeney, Turnbull and Hough 2008, p.30).

The results from the British pilot evaluations showed that those completing DTTOs (i.e. having run their full course or terminating early for good progress) were significantly less likely to be reconvicted than those not. In the English schemes 53% of completers were reconvicted of another offence within two years compared with 91% of non-completers (Hough *et al.* 2003). In Scotland, reconviction rates stood at 52% for completers and 79% for non-completers (McIvor 2004). While these findings are consistent with other studies showing that completion of substance misuse programmes is associated with reduced rates of reconviction (Hollis 2007),[2] regional variations in DTTO performance persist. For example, in 2004/5 completion rates for DTTOs ranged from 10% in North Yorkshire to 52% in Dyfed/Powys (National Probation Service 2005, p.17). This variation in DTTO completion rates is likely to have been the result of a number of interrelated factors: treatment availability and quality (including its setting and orientation) being prominent among these (McSweeney, Turnbull and Hough 2008, p.33).

Nevertheless between 2002 and 2006 DTTO completion rates in England and Wales rose from 25 to 59% (Ministry of Justice 2007, p.53). In fact, these figures for 2006 compare favourably with completion rates for Scottish DTTOs (38%) (Scottish Government 2007, p.58) and structured treatment services in England (52%) during the same period (NTA 2008, p.39). More recent one-year reconviction rates for DTTOs in England and Wales also fell from 79% in 2002 to 70% in 2005 (there were reductions in the frequency of offending during this period too) (Ministry of Justice 2008, p.21).

---

2   Though it is not clear to what extent these reductions in reoffending are related to treatment
     interventions or to differences between completers and non-completers.

Moreover, the 12-month reconviction rate for the DTTO cohort in 2005 is lower than the recent figures reported for both users accessing mainstream treatment as part of NTORS (74%) (Gossop *et al.* 2006) and sub-samples of drug-using offenders on supervision by the prison and probation services (74–5%) (Howard 2006; May, Sharma and Stewart 2008). In fact, the rate at which drug-misusing offenders are reconvicted appears to have changed little over the last 15 years (May 1999).[3]

Key findings from the QCT Europe study

There is very little research evidence outside the US to demonstrate the effectiveness of 'coerced' forms of treatment relative to 'voluntary' ones. However, one notable recent exception is the QCT Europe study.

This research involved parallel studies in Austria, England, Germany, Italy and Switzerland and sampled respondents from 65 purposively selected treatment centres between June 2003 and May 2004 (representing a mix of community-based and in-patient services). Independent researchers recruited a random sample of 845 people who had entered these services – just over half (n=427) of them had done so as part of a court order – and tracked their progress at four intervals over an 18-month period using a standardized and validated research instrument (the European Addiction Severity Index).

The study also drew on in-depth qualitative interview data with a total of 84 health and criminal justice professionals from across these sites and 138 of those from the quantitative sample accessing 'coerced' treatment. The English component of the study tracked a cohort of 157 people who had entered community-based drug treatment at one of ten research sites across London and Kent between June 2003 and January 2004; three-fifths (n=89) having done so as part of a DTTO. Full results from both the English (McSweeney *et al.* 2007) and the overall study (Uchtenhagen *et al.* 2008) have been reported elsewhere. Readers are advised to refer to these peer-reviewed papers for full details of the methodology employed, approach to data analysis and findings from the research.

The English results (which replicated those from the other four partner countries involved in the QCT Europe study) revealed statistically

---

3   Using data on just under 7500 offenders commencing a community penalty in six probation areas during 1993, May observed that 71% of those with drug problems were reconvicted compared with 45% of other offenders (1999, p.2).

significant and sustained reductions in self-reported illicit drug use and offending behaviours over an 18-month follow-up period for both the 'coerced' and 'voluntary' groups. These reductions were maintained when adjustments were made for missing data and time at reduced risk. The largest reductions across the follow-up period were observed in the 'coerced' group, reflecting their poor prognosis across a number of the domains measured at intake to treatment.

Figure 11.1, for example, indicates that among the English sample significant reductions in self-reported crime were sustained when adjustments were made for time at reduced risk (i.e. during periods of imprisonment or in-patient treatment). This approach provides a ratio for days involved in crime during the previous month as a proportion of days at liberty in the community to offend.

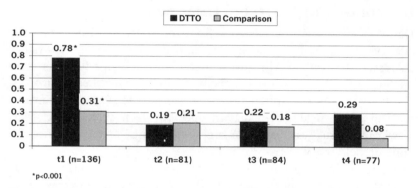

Figure 11.1 Self-reported days involved in crime during the last month as a proportion of days, by group

There were commensurate reductions in self-reported use of and expenditure on illicit drugs too: from a median of £1200 in the 30 days before intake interview (n=156) to £30 (n=104) at six-month follow-up. Whilst there were significant reductions in self-reported risk behaviours (e.g. sharing injecting equipment) and improvements in housing and personal relationships, there were only modest improvements in mental health and no change in very high rates of unemployment (which stood at 78% at the end of the follow-up period). Overall, though, there were no significant differences observed between those 'coerced' into drug treatment and the comparison group of 'volunteers' accessing support through non-CJS routes in retention rates and other outcomes.

The findings from the study have led the authors to conclude that 'coerced' treatment approaches could be considered viable alternatives to imprisonment and a vehicle for *initiating* recovery and desistance processes. For instance, recent British data indicates that up to 70% of those using heroin in the month prior to imprisonment report continued use while in custody (Strang *et al.* 2006) and most problem drug users fail to sustain any behaviour changes made while in custody upon release (data from one UK study reported a 75% relapse rate among released prisoners) (Bullock 2003). Furthermore, non-custodial treatment alternatives are likely to be a more cost-effective approach and have fewer detrimental effects (UKDPC 2008).

Barriers that inhibit recovery and desistance within the context of 'coerced' treatment

Despite some promising evidence from the study to demonstrate the effectiveness of DTTOs as a means of initiating recovery and desistance processes, the research also revealed considerable scope for improving methods of delivery to further facilitate and sustain these outcomes. While these points are of course specific to the DTTO (which towards the end of the fieldwork had been operational for six years) it seems reasonable to suggest that these issues will also be of relevance for the ongoing delivery of DRRs.

A key theme apparent throughout the study was the need to refine referral and assessment processes further. Efforts in this direction were often hampered for a range of reasons. Prominent among these was the difficulty of accurately assessing motivation (for genuine behaviour change as well as for treatment) and identifying those likely to do well. Qualitative interview data with professionals indicated that these endeavours were in turn hindered by the pressures of commencement targets and a pervasive performance management culture, and ongoing structural and organizational change.

Despite some substantial investment and expansion of drug treatment provision in England in the period since the introduction of DTTOs, it seemed that providing appropriate, responsive treatment options in a timely manner could still prove problematic. Similar issues were raised during the piloting of both English and Scottish DTTO schemes (Eley *et al.* 2002; Turnbull *et al.* 2000). Removing these particular barriers will require, among other things, more of a focus on provision for stimulant users, who are over-represented in CJS caseloads (Jones *et al.* 2007), women, young people and drug-misusing offenders from Black and minority ethnic groups (see also UKDPC 2008).

Inconsistencies around procedures for drug testing, court reviews and enforcing DTTO conditions emerged as important obstacles hampering efforts aimed at promoting recovery and desistance within this particular context. There were consistent calls for greater clarity around the aims and rationale for the frequency of testing, the consequences of failed tests and how drug testing should be used to complement care plans. In relation to the DTTO review process concerns tended to focus on the continuity, style and quality of interaction between participants during reviews and the limited scope within existing legislation for discretion in responding constructively to non-compliance (see McSweeney *et al.* 2008).

Finally, effective arrangements for aftercare and reintegration beyond the period of supervision often appeared to be absent or superficial across the ten English sites considered as part of the QCT Europe study (this was also largely true for those accessing treatment via non-CJS routes). This was a reflection of the limited capacity more broadly within both the CJS and drug treatment services to address and tackle wider social and environmental factors which serve as barriers to recovery and desistance processes, such as relationships, housing and employment.

Conclusions

Following their introduction in Britain as pilot schemes a decade ago, there is now a reasonable body of evidence to demonstrate the effectiveness of one particular form of 'coerced' treatment, in the shape of DTTOs, in reducing illicit drug use and offending for a significant minority of those drug-misusing offenders exposed to them. While more research is clearly required (e.g. to establish which particular treatment approaches and settings work best for whom) there may also be grounds for cautious optimism about the capacity of these measures to initiate recovery and desistance processes. Nevertheless, what research evidence we have at our disposal clearly identifies the considerable scope for further refinement to the way in which CJS-based treatment is implemented and delivered in order to sustain these processes over the long term. This includes ensuring that more effective, responsive and integrated forms of support are consistently delivered to drug-misusing offenders both during and after a period of CJS supervision.[4]

References

Bennett, T., Holloway, K. and Farrington, D. (2008) 'The statistical association between drug misuse and crime: A meta-analysis.' *Aggression and Violent Behavior 13*, 107–118.

Best, D., Day, E. and Morgan, B. (2006) *Addiction Careers and the Natural History of Change*. Research briefing 20. London: National Treatment Agency.

Best, D.W., Ghufran, S., Day, E., Ray, R. and Loaring, J. (2008) 'Breaking the habit: A retrospective analysis of desistance factors among formerly problematic heroin users.' *Drug and Alcohol Review 27*, 619–624.

Buchanan, J. (2004) 'Missing links: Problem drug use and social exclusion.' *Probation Journal 51*, 387–397.

Bullock, T. (2003) 'Changing levels of drug use before, during and after imprisonment.' In M. Ramsay (ed.) *Prisoners' Drug Use and Treatment: Seven Research Studies*. Home Office Research Study 267. London: Home Office.

Burnett, R. and McNeill, F. (2005) 'The place of the officer–offender relationship in assisting offenders to desist from crime.' *Probation Journal 52*, 221–242.

Eley, S., Gallop, K., McIvor, G., Morgan, K. and Yates, R. (2002) *Drug Treatment and Testing Orders: Evaluation of the Scottish Pilots*. Edinburgh: Scottish Executive Central Research Unit.

Farabee, D., Prendergast, M. and Anglin, M.D. (1998) 'The effectiveness of coerced drug treatment for drug-abusing offenders.' *Federal Probation 62*, 3–11.

Farrall, S. (2002) *Rethinking What Works with Offenders*. Cullompton: Willan.

Farrington, D., Coid, J., Harnett, L., Jolliffe, D. *et al.* (2006) *Criminal Careers and Life Successes: New Findings from the Cambridge Study in Delinquent Development*. Home Office Research Findings 281. London: Home Office.

Gossop, M., Marsden, J., Stewart, D. and Kidd, T. (2003) 'The National Treatment Outcome Research Study (NTORS): 4–5 year follow-up results.' *Addiction 98*, 291–303.

Gossop, M., Trakada, K., Stewart, D. and Witton, J. (2005) 'Reductions in criminal convictions after addiction treatment: 5-year follow-up.' *Drug and Alcohol Dependence 79*, 295–302.

Gossop, M., Trakada, K., Stewart, D. and Witton, J. (2006) *Levels of Conviction following Drug Treatment: Linking Data from the National Treatment Outcome Research Study and the Offenders Index*. Home Office Research Findings 275. London: Home Office.

---

4   I would like to acknowledge the significant work and contribution of colleagues from the various partner institutions and the numerous agencies which facilitated access to their staff and clients as part of the QCT study; in particular: Alex Stevens (project coordinator, University of Kent), Neil Hunt (University of Kent) and Paul Turnbull (King's College London).

   The QCT Europe study was funded by the Fifth European Community Framework Programme Research, Technological Development and Demonstration Activities (Quality of Life Programme, contract number QLG4-CT-2002-01446).

   The author is solely responsible for the content of this paper. It does not represent the opinion of the Community nor necessarily the other *QCT Europe* partners. Furthermore, the Community is not responsible for any use that might be made of data appearing in this paper.

   Further details of the Institute for Criminal Policy Research are available at: www.kcl. ac.uk/icpr.

   For more information about the *QCT Europe* study visit: www.kent.ac.uk/eiss/projects/ qcteurope/index.html.

Harper, R. and Hardy, S. (2000) 'An evaluation of motivational interviewing as a method of intervention with clients in a probation setting.' *British Journal of Social Work 30*, 393–400.

Hearnden, I. and Harocopos, A. (1999) *Problem Drug Use and Probation in London.* Home Office Research Findings 112. London: Home Office.

Hollis, V. (2007) *Reconviction Analysis of Programme Data using Interim Accredited Programmes Software (IAPS).* London: RDS/NOMS.

Holloway, K., Bennett, T. and Farrington, D. (2005) *The Effectiveness of Criminal Justice and Treatment Programmes in Reducing Drug-Related Crime: A Systematic Review.* Home Office Online Report 26/05. London: Home Office.

Hough, M., Clancy, A., McSweeney, T. and Turnbull, P.J. (2003) *The Impact of Drug Treatment and Testing Orders on Offending: Two Year Reconviction Results.* Home Office Research Findings 184. London: Home Office.

Howard, P. (2006) *The Offender Assessment System: An Evaluation of the Second Pilot.* Home Office Research Findings 278. London: Home Office.

Hser, Y., Longshore, D. and Anglin, M.D. (2007) 'The life course perspective on drug use: A conceptual framework for understanding drug use trajectories.' *Evaluation Review 31*, 515–547.

Hunt, N. and Stevens, A. (2004) 'Whose harm? Harm and the shift from health to coercion in UK drug policy.' *Social Policy and Society 3*, 333–342.

Jones, A., Weston, S., Moody, A., Millar, T., Dollin, L., Anderson, T. and Donmall, M. (2007) *The Drug Treatment Outcomes Research Study (DTORS): Baseline Report.* Home Office Research Report 3. London: Home Office.

Maguire, M. and Raynor, P. (2006) 'How the resettlement of prisoners promotes desistance from crime: Or does it?' *Criminology and Criminal Justice 6*, 1, 19–38.

Maruna, S. and Farrall, S. (2004) 'Desistance from crime: A theoretical reformulation.' *Kolner Zeitschrift fur Soziologie und Sozialpsychologie 43*, 171–194.

May, C. (1999) *The Role of Social Factors in Predicting Reconviction for Offenders on Community Penalties.* Home Office Research Findings No. 97. London: Home Office.

May, C., Sharma, N. and Stewart, D. (2008) *Factors Linked to Re-offending: A One-year Follow-up of Prisoners Who Took Part in the Resettlement Surveys 2001, 2003 and 2004.* Research Summary 5. London: Ministry of Justice.

McIvor, G. (2004) *Reconviction Following Drug Treatment and Testing Orders.* Edinburgh: Scottish Executive.

McNeill, F., Batchelor, S., Burnett, R. and Knox, J. (2005) *21st Century Social Work: Reducing Re-offending: Key Practice Skills.* Glasgow: Glasgow School of Social Work.

McSweeney, T., Stevens, A., Hunt, N. and Turnbull, P.J. (2007) 'Twisting arms or a helping hand? Assessing the impact of "coerced" and comparable "voluntary" drug treatment options.' *British Journal of Criminology 47*, 470–490.

McSweeney, T., Stevens, A., Hunt, N. and Turnbull, P.J. (2008) 'Drug testing and court review hearings: Uses and limitations.' *Probation Journal 55*, 1, 39–53.

McSweeney, T., Turnbull, P.J. and Hough, M. (2008) *The Treatment and Supervision of Drug-Dependent Offenders: A Review of the Literature Prepared for the UK Drug Policy Commission.* London: UK Drug Policy Commission.

Ministry of Justice (2007) *Offender Management Caseload Statistics 2006. Statistical Bulletin.* London: Ministry of Justice.

Ministry of Justice (2008) *Re-offending of Adults: New Measures of Re-offending 2000–2005, England and Wales.* Statistics bulletin. London: Ministry of Justice.

National Probation Service (2005) *Performance Report 16 and Weighted Scorecard 2004/05.* London: Home Office.

National Treatment Agency for Substance Misuse (NTA) (2008) *Statistics from the National Drug Treatment Monitoring System (NDTMS) 1 April 2007–31 March 2008.* London: NTA.

Parker, H. (2004) 'The new drugs interventions industry: What outcomes can drugs/criminal justice treatment programmes realistically deliver?' *Probation Journal 51*, 379–386.

Prendergast, M.L., Podus, D., Chang, E. and Urada, D. (2002) 'The effectiveness of drug abuse treatment: A meta-analysis of comparison group studies.' *Drug and Alcohol Dependence 67*, 53–72.

Schroeder, R.D., Giordano, P.C. and Cernkovich, S.A. (2007) 'Drug use and desistance processes.' *Criminology 45*, 1, 191–222.

Scottish Government (2007) *Criminal Justice Social Work Statistics, 2006–07*. Edinburgh: Scottish Government.

Seddon, T. (2006) 'Drugs, crime and social exclusion: Social context and social theory in British drugs–crime research.' *British Journal of Criminology 46*, 680–703.

Seddon, T. (2007) 'Coerced drug treatment in the criminal justice system: Conceptual, ethical and criminological issues.' *Criminology and Criminal Justice 7*, 269–286.

Seddon, T., Ralphs, R. and Williams, L. (2008) 'Risk, security and the "criminalization" of British drug policy.' *British Journal of Criminology 48*, 818–834.

Stevens, A., Berto, D., Heckmann, W., Kerschl, V., Oeuvray, K., van Ooyen, M., Steffan, E. and Uchtenhagen, A. (2005a) 'Quasi-compulsory treatment of drug dependent offenders: An international literature review.' *Substance Use and Misuse 40*, 269–283.

Stevens, A. (2007) 'When two dark figures collide: Evidence and discourse on drug-related crime.' *Critical Social Policy 27*, 77–99.

Stevens, A., McSweeney, T., van Ooyen, M. and Uchtenhagen, A. (2005b) 'Editorial: On coercion.' *International Journal of Drug Policy 16*, 207–209.

Stimson, G.V. (2000) 'Blair declares war: The unhealthy state of British drug policy.' *International Journal of Drug Policy 11*, 259–264.

Strang, J., Gossop, M., Heuston, J., Green, J., Whiteley, C. and Maden, A. (2006) 'Persistence of drug use during imprisonment: Relationship of drug type, recency of use and severity of dependence to use of heroin, cocaine and amphetamine in prison.' *Addiction 101*, 1125–1132.

Turnbull, P.J., McSweeney, T., Hough, M., Webster, R. and Edmunds, M. (2000) *Drug Treatment and Testing Orders: Final Evaluation Report*. Home Office Research Study 212. London: Home Office.

Uchtenhagen, A., Stevens, A., Berto, D., Frick, U. *et al.* (2008) 'Evaluation of therapeutic alternatives to imprisonment for drug dependent offenders: Experience from a comparative European multi-country study.' *Heroin Addiction and Related Clinical Problems 10*, 5–10.

UK Drug Policy Commission (UKDPC) (2008) *Reducing Drug Use, Reducing Reoffending: Are Programmes for Problem Drug-Using Offenders in the UK Supported by the Evidence?* London: UKDPC.

Weaver, B. and McNeill, F. (2007) *Giving Up Crime: Directions for Policy*. Glasgow: The Scottish Consortium on Crime and Criminal Justice.

White, W.L. (2007) 'Addiction recovery: Its definition and conceptual boundaries.' *Journal of Substance Abuse Treatment 33*, 229–241.

CHAPTER 12

Some Concluding Thoughts

Margaret S. Malloch and Rowdy Yates

This book set out to highlight some of the emerging and some of the more entrenched issues surrounding the current recovery agenda. The majority of chapters testify to a more optimistic climate for service development and delivery, perhaps presenting a challenge to the traditionally low expectations that would appear to characterize service user outcomes as held by service providers, outlined by Best (Chapter 2), Thom (Chapter 4) and De Leon (Chapter 5). The acknowledgement that 'recovery' can play a key role in service provision seems to have introduced an element of optimism and hope into certain services. This is outlined by Kuladharini (Chapter 3) where she considers how developments that transformed one project in Glasgow also had a potential to spread that optimism and hope into the wider community, providing an opportunity to inspire service providers, members of the community, friends and families affected by drug and alcohol problems, and the individual and/or service user.

There is a generally shared view from all the contributors that in order to support people in recovery it is essential to build social capital through empowering the individual and supporting groups and communities around them. This is highlighted throughout the book in discussions about service provision (Chapters 2 and 3) and therapeutic communities as a way of supporting individual change (Chapters 5 and 6). Thom provides a cautionary note when she acknowledges the need to avoid imposing values and lifestyles on individuals which they have tried to escape from in the first place, for example encouraging women to comply with limiting roles (see Chapter 4). While 'recovery' and 'treatment' are not seen as incompatible in the main, there is a recognition that the empowerment of the individual client is also likely to require a reduction of professional power. This is not without contention, however.

Supporting recovery also requires appropriate resources directed towards alleviating social exclusion and enhancing the opportunities available to groups and individuals. This means more than simply providing 'treatment' options; it suggests a more fundamental shift to building or rebuilding communities, and providing real alternatives for the individuals and groups within them.

Our contributors to the 'voices of recovery' section of this book are unambiguous in their descriptions of the changes that have been made to their lives 'in recovery' which they describe as a point in time when they entered a new phase of living, where their spirit was rekindled and a process of change was initiated. Several of the contributors describe how this inspired them to come to see a meaning in their lives and to enact that meaning through work with others. One of the real challenges facing the 'recovery agenda' is how this work is recognized and acknowledged. The current emphasis on professional provision often relegates the work undertaken by mutual aid and self-help groups as secondary or problematic (although this does appear to be changing). However, without the support of official bodies (i.e. Drug and Alcohol Action Teams (DAATs)), small, non-professional projects are often required to struggle on with minimal funding. Others (notably Alcoholics Anonymous (AA) and Narcotics Anonymous (NA)) will not accept funds, maintaining the tradition of self-support as a way of retaining independence and freedom from the constraints imposed by funders. This can often mean that provisions which appear eminently successful on their own terms are not recognized as such by policy makers (see David Bryce in Chapter 8, De Leon in Chapter 5). Different (and potentially unconventional) ways of working are too frequently dismissed as not cost effective or unable to provide sufficient 'evidence' of success. The adoption of a 'recovery agenda' requires new ways to define and measure what works, and to allow for creativity in the provision of support. It also needs to be long term and ongoing. As all our 'voices of recovery' contributors highlight, their recovery is a key life experience that is without limit of time. How this is captured remains a challenge to researchers and service-commissioners. But it is undeniable that the changes described in Chapter 8 (in behaviour, self-awareness, emotions, values and spiritual well-being) can and do occur in the lives of many individuals, often, but not always, outwith the boundaries of professional interventions. There is evidence, growing all the time, that individuals can and do recover from addiction. While the 'recovery agenda' is not without its critics – and still remains in many ways somewhat ethereal – the potential for a positive and inspiring change to practice and policy is worth pursuing. Scotland is taking a major step in this direction and will be worth closer examination in the future.

Contributors

David Best, Reader in Criminal Justice at the University of the West of Scotland, is a Chartered Psychologist and Criminologist who has worked in addictions research at the University of Strathclyde, Institute of Psychiatry and the University of Birmingham. Additionally, he has worked in research policy at the National Treatment Agency. His recent work is around systems modelling for drug treatment and in mapping the recovery movement in the UK. He is chair of the UK Recovery Academy.

Wendy Dawson is Chief Executive of the Ley Community, a residential drug/alcohol residential therapeutic community in Oxfordshire. She has worked for Barnardos North East; NECA (North East Council on Addictions); Newcastle Upon Tyne YMCA; YWCA; and Connexions North London. She was formerly the developer and lead lecturer on Ruskin College, Oxford's Foundation Degree in Youth and Community Work.

George De Leon, PhD, is an internationally recognized expert in the treatment of substance abuse, and acknowledged as the leading authority on treatment and research in therapeutic communities. He is senior scientist and former Director of the Center for Therapeutic Community Research, and currently Science Director of the Behavior Science Training programme at National Development and Research Institutes, Inc. (NDRI). He is Clinical Professor of Psychiatry, Division of Alcoholism and Drug Abuse, at New York University Medical School.

Mark Gilman is the North West Regional Manager of the National Treatment Agency for Substance Misuse in England. He has a first degree in Organization Theory and an MA in the study of Drugs, Crime and Social Deviance. He has been working with problem drug users since the 1970s and in 1984 was a Research Associate investigating Heroin Use and Young People in the North of England. He has worked at the Lifeline Project, both as manager of one of the first Community Drug Teams in Greater Manchester, and subsequently, as the North West Regional Drug Prevention Manager and Director of Research.

Brian Kidd is a front-line Consultant Psychiatrist working for NHS Tayside's Substance Misuse Services and is Clinical Senior Lecturer in Addiction Psychiatry at the University of Dundee. He has been a Scottish Advisory Council on Drug

Misuse (SACDM) member since 1998 and has led key working groups advising government on care and treatment for substance misusers in Scotland. From 2005 to 2009 he was Chair of the Dundee City Drug and Alcohol Action Team (DAAT). In 2007 he was a member of the specialist group updating the UK national Treatment Guidelines. In 2008 he was invited by the UK Drug Policy Commission (UKDPC) to participate in the consensus group producing a definition of recovery. In 2009 he was invited to chair the Scottish Drug Strategy Delivery Commission.

Dharmacarini Kuladharini (previously known as Sophia Young) is currently the Service Manager for South East Alternatives, a Community Rehabilitation Service based in the Gorbals, Glasgow. Prior to this she set up and managed the 218 Service for women offenders in Glasgow and a young person's drug and alcohol service in Falkirk.

Margaret Malloch is a Senior Research Fellow in the Scottish Centre for Crime and Justice Research, University of Stirling. Her key research interests include an examination of responses to 'drug-related crime'; the experiences of women drug users in prison and the community; and 'holistic', community-based responses to crime and social exclusion.

Tim McSweeney is a Senior Research Fellow at the Institute for Criminal Policy Research based at King's College London. He has ten years' experience of conducting and managing social science research with local, national and international dimensions using both quantitative and qualitative methodologies. His research activities to date have focused on substance misuse, its treatment and the role played by criminal justice interventions in tackling these and related issues. He has served as an advisor on 'coerced' drug treatment options to both the Council of Europe and UN Office on Drugs and Crime.

Betsy Thom is Professor of Health Policy at Middlesex University. She is a sociologist, specializing in research on alcohol and drugs and with an interest in gender issues. Current studies include work on community responses to problem alcohol/drug use, 'partnership' working and cross-national studies on alcohol consumption in Europe. She is the editor-in-chief of the journal Drugs: Education, Prevention and Policy.

Rowdy Yates is Senior Research Fellow and facilitator of the Scottish Addiction Studies group in the Department of Applied Social Science, University of Stirling. He has worked in the drugs field for more than 35 years and, prior to this appointment, he was the Director and co-founder of the Lifeline Project; one of the longest established drug specialist services in the UK. He is Executive Director of EWODOR (the European Working Group on Drugs Oriented Research), Vice-President (Teaching and Research) of the EFTC (European Federation of Therapeutic Communities) and Chair, Addictions Reference Group, Royal College of Psychiatrists (Community of Communities).

Albert Zandvoort, BA Hons, MA, PhD, DLit et Phil, is the Founder and Chief Executive of the Bayberry Community, a therapeutic community for addicted health professionals in Oxfordshire, UK. Albert has qualifications in modern literature, education and psychotherapy and has worked as a professor of leadership studies, corporate executive and professional soldier. He has published books and articles on spirituality, leadership, language teaching and political poetry.

Subject Index

Author Index